MW00953735

NINJA AIR FRYER PRO 4-IN-1 COOKBOOK

100 Complete Mind-blowing Recipes for Beginners & Advanced Users to Air fry, Roast, Reheat & Dehydrate your Favorite Meals. Including 2-Week Meal Plan

Eva Williams

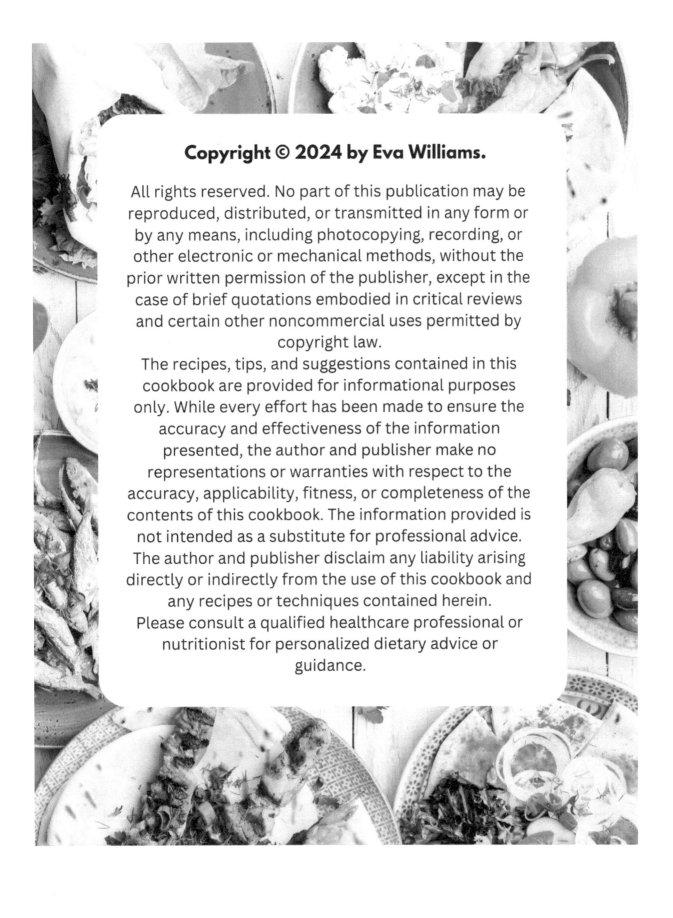

Copyright © 2024 by Eva Williams.

All rights reserved. No part of this publication may be reproduced, distributed, or transmitted in any form or by any means, including photocopying, recording, or other electronic or mechanical methods, without the prior written permission of the publisher, except in the case of brief quotations embodied in critical reviews and certain other noncommercial uses permitted by copyright law.

The recipes, tips, and suggestions contained in this cookbook are provided for informational purposes only. While every effort has been made to ensure the accuracy and effectiveness of the information presented, the author and publisher make no representations or warranties with respect to the accuracy, applicability, fitness, or completeness of the contents of this cookbook. The information provided is not intended as a substitute for professional advice. The author and publisher disclaim any liability arising directly or indirectly from the use of this cookbook and any recipes or techniques contained herein.

Please consult a qualified healthcare professional or nutritionist for personalized dietary advice or guidance.

Table of Contents

INTRODUCTION

Welcome to the world of the Ninja Air Fryer Pro, where culinary possibilities meet innovative technology. If you've ever craved the crispy, golden-brown texture of fried foods without the guilt of excess oil, you're in for a treat. The Ninja Air Fryer Pro is more than just a kitchen gadget; it's a game-changer for both novice cooks and seasoned chefs.

Imagine preparing your favorite meals with ease, speed, and a fraction of the fat traditionally used in frying. With the Ninja Air Fryer Pro, you can achieve this and more. This versatile appliance combines the power of air frying, roasting, reheating, and dehydrating, offering a comprehensive solution for all your cooking needs. From crispy French fries and succulent chicken wings to perfectly roasted vegetables and deliciously chewy dried fruits, the Ninja Air Fryer Pro does it all.

The secret behind its exceptional performance lies in its advanced Air Crisp Technology. At the heart of this technology is a 400°F superheated air system that surrounds your food, ensuring even cooking and delivering that sought-after crunch with little to no oil. This means you can enjoy your favorite fried foods with up to 75% less fat than traditional frying methods. Healthier eating has never been so satisfying or so delicious.

Capacity is another standout feature of the Ninja Air Fryer Pro. With its generous 5-quart nonstick basket and crisper plate, you can cook up to 4 pounds of French fries or 5 pounds of chicken wings in one go. This makes it perfect for family meals, parties, or simply preparing a week's worth of healthy snacks in one batch. The space-saving design ensures that this powerhouse fits comfortably on your countertop without compromising on cooking capacity.

Whether you're preparing frozen foods or fresh ingredients, the Ninja Air Fryer Pro brings convenience to your kitchen. Its fast cooking times mean you can go from frozen to crispy in mere minutes, making it ideal for busy weeknights or impromptu gatherings. Plus, the easy-to-clean nonstick components simplify the post-meal cleanup process, so you can spend more time enjoying your culinary creations and less time scrubbing dishes.

This cookbook is your gateway to mastering the Ninja Air Fryer Pro. Inside, you'll find 100 mind-blowing recipes that showcase the versatility of this remarkable appliance. From breakfast delights and poultry perfection to vegetarian dishes and delectable desserts, each recipe is designed to help you make the most of your air fryer. Whether you're a beginner just starting out or an advanced user looking to expand your culinary repertoire, these recipes will guide you step-by-step to create mouthwatering meals with ease.

So, get ready to embark on a culinary adventure. The Ninja Air Fryer Pro is here to transform your cooking experience, making it healthier, faster, and more enjoyable. Let's dive in and discover the endless possibilities that await in the world of air frying, roasting, reheating, and dehydrating. Welcome to a new era of delicious, guilt-free cooking!

GETTING STARTED

Unboxing Your Ninja Air Fryer Pro

Welcome to the exciting first step of your culinary journey with the Ninja Air Fryer Pro. Unboxing this innovative kitchen appliance is the beginning of many delicious and healthier meals. Let's walk through what you'll find inside the box and how to get started.

Parts and Accessories

As you open the box, you'll find the following components neatly packed:

1. **Ninja Air Fryer Pro Unit**: The main body of the air fryer with a digital control panel.
2. **5-Quart Nonstick Basket**: This large-capacity basket is designed to hold a significant amount of food, perfect for family meals.
3. **Crisper Plate**: Fits inside the basket and helps achieve that crispy texture by allowing hot air to circulate underneath the food.
4. **Chef-Inspired 20 Recipe Book**: A handy guide to get you started with delicious recipes specifically designed for your Ninja Air Fryer Pro.
5. **Cooking Charts**: These charts provide recommended cooking times and temperatures for various foods, ensuring perfect results every time.

Initial Setup and Safety Tips

Before you start cooking, it's important to set up your Ninja Air Fryer Pro correctly and understand some essential safety tips.

Initial Setup

1. **Remove Packaging**: Carefully remove all packaging materials from the unit and its components. Ensure you've taken out all parts listed in the parts and accessories section.
2. **Clean the Components**: Wash the nonstick basket and crisper plate with warm, soapy water. Rinse and dry them thoroughly. Wipe the exterior and interior of the air fryer unit with a damp cloth.
3. **Assemble the Air Fryer**: Place the crisper plate inside the nonstick basket. Slide the basket into the main unit until it clicks into place.
4. **Place the Air Fryer on a Flat Surface**: Ensure the unit is on a stable, heat-resistant surface with at least 5 inches of space around it for proper ventilation.

Safety Tips

1. **Read the Manual**: Familiarize yourself with the user manual that comes with your Ninja Air Fryer Pro. It contains important information about operating the appliance safely.
2. **Electrical Safety**: Ensure the power cord is plugged into a grounded outlet. Do not use extension cords or power strips. Avoid placing the air fryer near water or other liquids.
3. **Hot Surfaces**: The air fryer becomes hot during use. Always use oven mitts or heat-resistant gloves when handling the basket or crisper plate. Avoid touching the exterior surfaces during operation.

4. **Proper Ventilation**: Ensure the air fryer is placed in a well-ventilated area. Do not block the air intake or exhaust vents, as proper airflow is crucial for safe and efficient operation.
5. **Unplug When Not in Use**: Always unplug the air fryer when it's not in use or before cleaning it. This prevents accidental starts and ensures your safety.

By carefully unboxing and setting up your Ninja Air Fryer Pro, you're ready to embark on a journey of healthier, tastier meals. With these initial steps and safety tips, you can confidently explore the versatile capabilities of your new kitchen companion.

How to Use the Ninja Air Fryer Pro
Basic Controls and Settings

Getting to know the basic controls and settings of your Ninja Air Fryer Pro is essential for mastering its use. Here's a quick guide to help you navigate the control panel and make the most of your air fryer.

1. **Power Button**: Located at the top of the control panel, the power button turns the unit on and off.
2. **Function Buttons**: These buttons allow you to select the desired cooking mode. Options typically include Air Fry, Roast, Reheat, and Dehydrate. Press the corresponding button to choose your cooking function.
3. **Temperature Control**: Use the up and down arrows to adjust the cooking temperature. The temperature range usually varies depending on the function selected, allowing precise control for different recipes.
4. **Time Control**: Use the up and down arrows to set the cooking time. The timer counts down as your food cooks, and the unit will automatically shut off once the timer reaches zero.
5. **Start/Pause Button**: After setting the desired temperature and time, press this button to start the cooking process. Press it again to pause cooking if needed.
6. **Display Screen**: The digital display shows the selected temperature, time, and cooking function. It also indicates the preheating process and cooking progress.
7. **Preset Buttons**: Some models feature preset buttons for common foods like French fries, chicken, and vegetables. These presets simplify the cooking process by automatically setting the ideal temperature and time.

Preheating and Cooking Tips

For optimal results with your Ninja Air Fryer Pro, follow these preheating and cooking tips:

Preheating

1. **Importance of Preheating**: Preheating ensures that the air fryer reaches the desired temperature before you start cooking, resulting in even and consistent cooking.
2. **How to Preheat**: Select the desired cooking function, temperature, and time. Press the Start/Pause button, and the air fryer will begin to preheat. Some models have a dedicated preheat function or indicator to signal when the unit is ready.

Cooking Tips

1. **Use Little to No Oil**: The Ninja Air Fryer Pro is designed to cook with minimal oil. A light spray or brush of oil on your food can enhance crispiness without adding unnecessary calories.
2. **Avoid Overcrowding**: For best results, arrange food in a single layer in the basket or on the crisper plate. Overcrowding can lead to uneven cooking and reduce the effectiveness of the Air Crisp Technology.
3. **Shake or Flip**: For even cooking, shake the basket or flip the food halfway through the cooking time. This is especially important for smaller items like fries or nuggets.
4. **Monitor Progress**: Use the digital display to keep an eye on the cooking time and temperature. Adjust as needed based on the recipe and your personal preferences.
5. **Experiment with Settings**: Don't be afraid to experiment with different temperatures and times to achieve your desired level of crispiness and doneness.

Cleaning and Maintenance

Proper cleaning and maintenance of your Ninja Air Fryer Pro will ensure it continues to perform optimally and lasts for years. Here's how to keep your air fryer in top condition:

Cleaning

1. **Unplug and Cool Down**: Always unplug the air fryer and let it cool completely before cleaning.
2. **Clean the Basket and Crisper Plate**: Remove the basket and crisper plate. Wash them with warm, soapy water using a non-abrasive sponge or cloth. Both components are usually dishwasher safe, making cleanup even easier.
3. **Wipe the Exterior and Interior**: Use a damp cloth to wipe down the exterior and interior of the air fryer. Avoid using harsh chemicals or abrasive materials that could damage the surfaces.
4. **Clean the Heating Element**: Check the heating element for any food residue. If necessary, use a soft brush or cloth to gently clean it. Ensure the unit is completely dry before using it again.

Maintenance

1. **Regular Inspections**: Periodically check the power cord and plug for any signs of damage. Ensure that all parts are in good condition and functioning properly.
2. **Proper Storage**: When not in use, store your air fryer in a cool, dry place. Keep it covered or in its original packaging to protect it from dust and debris.
3. **Follow Manufacturer's Guidelines**: Adhere to the care and maintenance instructions provided in the user manual. This includes any specific recommendations for cleaning and handling your particular model.

By understanding the basic controls, preheating and cooking tips, and proper cleaning and maintenance, you'll be well-equipped to make the most of your Ninja Air Fryer Pro. Enjoy the journey to healthier, tastier meals with this versatile kitchen companion.

The Ninja Air Fryer Pro is not just an appliance; it's a revolution in your kitchen. Here are some of the standout benefits that make it an essential tool for any home cook:

1. **Healthier Cooking**: Enjoy your favorite fried foods with up to 75% less fat than traditional frying methods. The Air Crisp Technology uses little to no oil, ensuring you get that crispy texture without the added calories.
2. **Versatility**: With its 4-in-1 functionality, the Ninja Air Fryer Pro can air fry, roast, reheat, and dehydrate. This means you can create a wide variety of dishes, from crispy appetizers to succulent roasts and healthy snacks.
3. **Speed and Efficiency**: The powerful heating system and superheated air ensure that your food cooks quickly and evenly. Whether you're preparing a quick weeknight dinner or a feast for family and friends, the Ninja Air Fryer Pro saves you time in the kitchen.
4. **Large Capacity**: The 5-quart nonstick basket and crisper plate can accommodate up to 4 pounds of French fries or 5 pounds of chicken wings. This makes it ideal for cooking large batches, perfect for families or gatherings.
5. **Space-Saving Design**: Despite its large capacity, the Ninja Air Fryer Pro is designed to save space on your countertop. Its compact footprint ensures that it fits comfortably in your kitchen without taking up too much room.
6. **Easy to Clean**: The nonstick basket and crisper plate are easy to clean, making post-meal cleanup a breeze. Simply wipe down or place them in the dishwasher for hassle-free maintenance.

Overview of 4-in-1 Functionality

The Ninja Air Fryer Pro is designed to simplify your cooking experience with its 4-in-1 functionality:

1. **Air Fry**: Achieve perfectly crispy and golden-brown results with little to no oil. From French fries and chicken wings to vegetables and seafood, air frying offers a healthier alternative to traditional frying.
2. **Roast**: Roast meats, vegetables, and more to perfection. The even heat distribution ensures your food is cooked thoroughly, resulting in tender and flavorful dishes.
3. **Reheat**: Say goodbye to soggy leftovers. The Ninja Air Fryer Pro can reheat your meals to their original crispiness, making leftovers taste freshly made.
4. **Dehydrate**: Create healthy snacks like dried fruits, vegetable chips, and beef jerky. The dehydration function removes moisture from your food, preserving it without the need for additives or preservatives.

Understanding Air Crisp Technology

Air Crisp Technology is the heart of the Ninja Air Fryer Pro, delivering exceptional cooking results with less fat and fewer calories. Here's how it works:

- **Superheated Air**: The Air Fryer Pro uses a powerful heating element to generate 400°F superheated air. This hot air circulates rapidly around the food, ensuring even cooking on all sides.

- **Little to No Oil**: Unlike traditional frying methods that submerge food in oil, air frying uses just a tiny amount—or no oil at all. The superheated air mimics the effect of deep-frying, giving you the same crispy texture with a fraction of the fat.
- **Even Cooking**: The high-speed air circulation ensures that heat is distributed evenly throughout the cooking chamber. This means your food cooks uniformly, reducing the risk of undercooked or burnt spots.
- **Retains Moisture**: While the exterior of your food becomes crispy, the interior remains moist and tender. This is particularly important for meats and poultry, where you want a juicy inside and a crunchy outside.

By combining these elements, Air Crisp Technology allows you to enjoy your favorite fried foods in a healthier way. Whether you're air frying, roasting, reheating, or dehydrating, the Ninja Air Fryer Pro ensures your meals are delicious, nutritious, and guilt-free.

Air Frying Basics
The Science of Air Frying

Air frying is a revolutionary cooking method that delivers the crispy, delicious results of traditional frying without the need for excessive oil. At the heart of this technology is the Ninja Air Fryer Pro's advanced Air Crisp Technology. Understanding how this works and the health benefits it offers can help you make the most of your air frying experience.

How Air Crisp Technology Works

1. **Superheated Air Circulation**:
   - **Heating Element**: The Ninja Air Fryer Pro is equipped with a powerful heating element that rapidly heats the air inside the cooking chamber to temperatures up to 400°F.
   - **Fan**: A high-speed fan circulates this superheated air around the food. This ensures that the hot air reaches all surfaces of the food, cooking it evenly from all sides.
2. **Maillard Reaction**:
   - **Crisping Process**: The hot air interacts with the surface of the food, causing the Maillard reaction. This chemical reaction between amino acids and reducing sugars gives browned foods their distinctive flavor and crisp texture.
   - **Minimal Oil**: While traditional frying submerges food in oil to achieve crispiness, air frying uses little to no oil. The circulating hot air mimics the effects of deep frying, making the food crispy on the outside while keeping it moist inside.
3. **Perforated Basket and Crisper Plate**:
   - **Even Cooking**: The design of the basket and crisper plate allows hot air to flow freely around the food. The perforations ensure that the air reaches all parts of the food, enhancing the crisping process.
   - **Drip Tray**: Excess oil and fat drip away from the food into the bottom of the basket, further reducing the overall fat content of the meal.

Health Benefits of Air Frying

1. **Reduced Fat Content**:
   - **Less Oil**: Traditional deep frying requires submerging food in oil, which significantly increases the fat and calorie content. Air frying, on the other hand, uses little to no oil. This means you can enjoy your favorite fried foods with up to 75% less fat.
   - **Healthier Alternatives**: By using healthier oils (like olive or avocado oil) in minimal amounts, air frying provides a way to indulge in "fried" foods without the guilt.
2. **Lower Calorie Intake**:
   - **Calorie Reduction**: The significant reduction in oil usage directly translates to fewer calories in your meals. For those looking to manage their weight or maintain a healthier diet, air frying is an excellent alternative to traditional frying methods.
3. **Preservation of Nutrients**:
   - **Minimal Nutrient Loss**: The quick cooking time and lower temperatures compared to deep frying help preserve the nutrients in your food. Vegetables, in particular, retain more of their vitamins and minerals when air-fried.
   - **Healthy Cooking**: The Ninja Air Fryer Pro's even heat distribution ensures that food is cooked thoroughly, reducing the risk of undercooked areas which can harbor bacteria.
4. **Reduction of Harmful Compounds**:
   - **Less Acrylamide**: Traditional frying at high temperatures can produce harmful compounds like acrylamide, which is associated with certain health risks. Air frying significantly reduces the formation of these compounds, making it a safer cooking method.
5. **Versatility and Variety**:
   - **Diverse Cooking Options**: The Ninja Air Fryer Pro isn't just for "frying." Its ability to roast, reheat, and dehydrate makes it a versatile tool in the kitchen, allowing you to prepare a wide range of healthy meals.
   - **Healthy Snacks**: Use the dehydrate function to make nutritious snacks like dried fruits and vegetable chips, which are free from the additives and preservatives found in store-bought options.

By harnessing the science of Air Crisp Technology, the Ninja Air Fryer Pro offers a healthier, more efficient way to enjoy your favorite foods. Not only does it reduce fat and calorie intake, but it also preserves nutrients and reduces the formation of harmful compounds. Embrace the benefits of air frying and discover how this innovative technology can transform your cooking and eating habits for the better.

Tips for Perfect Air Frying

Achieving perfect results with your Ninja Air Fryer Pro involves more than just pressing a few buttons. Here are some expert tips to help you make the most of your air frying experience:

Choosing the Right Ingredients

1. **Fresh and High-Quality Ingredients**:
   - **Freshness**: Always use fresh ingredients for the best results. Fresh vegetables, meats, and seafood cook more evenly and retain their natural flavors.

- o **Quality**: Choose high-quality meats and seafood. Lean cuts of meat and fresh fish will cook more evenly and result in better textures and flavors.

2. **Appropriate Cuts and Sizes**:
   - o **Uniform Pieces**: Cut your ingredients into uniform sizes to ensure even cooking. For example, chop vegetables into similarly sized pieces and cut meats into similar thicknesses.
   - o **Avoid Overly Thick Pieces**: Thicker pieces of meat or vegetables may not cook evenly. If necessary, pound thicker cuts of meat to an even thickness for consistent cooking.

3. **Proper Coating and Seasoning**:
   - o **Light Oil Coating**: While air frying uses less oil, a light coating can help achieve a crispy texture. Use a sprayer to apply a thin layer of oil evenly over the food.
   - o **Seasoning**: Season your ingredients before air frying. Dry rubs, marinades, and herbs can enhance the flavor and help create a delicious crust.

4. **Frozen vs. Fresh**:
   - o **Frozen Foods**: Air frying is excellent for cooking frozen foods, but be mindful of the cooking times, which may need to be adjusted. Avoid overcrowding to ensure even cooking.
   - o **Fresh Foods**: Fresh ingredients often cook faster and may require lower temperatures than frozen counterparts. Always refer to cooking charts or guides for specific foods.

Best Practices for Even Cooking

1. **Avoid Overcrowding**:
   - o **Single Layer**: Arrange food in a single layer in the basket or on the crisper plate. Overcrowding can prevent hot air from circulating properly, leading to uneven cooking.
   - o **Batch Cooking**: If you have a large amount of food, cook in batches. This ensures each piece is evenly exposed to the hot air.

2. **Shake or Flip Midway**:
   - o **Shaking**: For smaller items like fries, nuggets, or vegetables, shake the basket halfway through the cooking process to ensure all sides cook evenly.
   - o **Flipping**: For larger items like chicken breasts or steaks, use tongs to flip the food halfway through the cooking time. This helps achieve even browning on both sides.

3. **Preheating the Air Fryer**:
   - o **Consistent Temperature**: Preheating the air fryer ensures it reaches the desired temperature before you start cooking. This helps in achieving consistent cooking results.
   - o **Quick Preheat**: Preheating usually takes just a few minutes. Set your desired temperature and time, then press start to preheat before adding your ingredients.

4. **Adjusting Temperature and Time**:
   - o **Monitor Progress**: Keep an eye on your food and adjust the temperature or time as needed. Every air fryer model may cook slightly differently, so it's essential to monitor the first few times you cook a new recipe.
   - o **Cooking Charts**: Refer to the cooking charts provided with your Ninja Air Fryer Pro for recommended temperatures and times for various foods. These guidelines help ensure optimal results.

5. **Proper Ventilation**:

- Air Circulation: Ensure there's adequate space around the air fryer for proper ventilation. This allows the unit to function efficiently and prevents overheating.
- Avoid Blocking Vents: Do not block the air intake and exhaust vents. Proper airflow is crucial for even cooking and the longevity of your appliance.

6. **Cleaning Between Batches**:
- Remove Residue: If cooking in multiple batches, clean out any crumbs or residue between batches. This prevents burning and smoking, which can affect the taste and quality of your food.
- Cooling Period: Allow the air fryer to cool slightly before wiping it out. This makes it safer to handle and more effective in removing any stuck-on food.

By choosing the right ingredients and following these best practices, you can achieve perfectly cooked, delicious meals every time with your Ninja Air Fryer Pro. Enjoy the convenience and health benefits of air frying while ensuring your food is always evenly cooked and bursting with flavor.

Troubleshooting and FAQs
Common Issues and Solutions

Even with the best equipment, sometimes things don't go as planned. Here's a troubleshooting guide to help you address common issues with your Ninja Air Fryer Pro, along with answers to frequently asked questions.

Troubleshooting Guide

1. **Food Isn't Crispy Enough**
- **Solution**: Ensure you're not overcrowding the basket. Cook in smaller batches to allow hot air to circulate properly. Lightly coat the food with oil to enhance crispiness.
2. **Food Is Overcooked or Burned**
- **Solution**: Reduce the cooking temperature or time. Refer to the cooking charts and adjust based on the size and type of food. Monitor the cooking process closely the first few times you try a new recipe.
3. **Food Isn't Cooked Evenly**
- **Solution**: Shake or flip the food halfway through the cooking process. Ensure the food is cut into uniform pieces and avoid overcrowding the basket.
4. **Air Fryer Won't Turn On**
- **Solution**: Check that the air fryer is plugged into a functioning power outlet. Ensure the basket is properly inserted into the unit, as some models won't operate if the basket isn't correctly in place. Verify that you're pressing the power button correctly.
5. **White Smoke Coming from the Air Fryer**
- **Solution**: White smoke usually indicates that there is excess oil or fat in the air fryer. Clean the basket and crisper plate to remove any grease or residue. Avoid using too much oil or cooking high-fat foods that can drip excessively.
6. **Black Smoke Coming from the Air Fryer**
- **Solution**: This could indicate that food has burned or that there are pieces of food stuck near the heating element. Turn off the air fryer, unplug it, and let it cool down. Clean the interior and remove any burnt food.
7. **Unit Is Making a Loud Noise**

- o **Solution**: A certain level of noise is normal due to the fan. However, if the noise is unusually loud, ensure that the unit is on a flat, stable surface and that nothing is obstructing the air vents. If the problem persists, contact customer support.

Frequently Asked Questions

1. **Can I Use Aluminum Foil or Parchment Paper in the Air Fryer?**
   - o **Answer**: Yes, you can use aluminum foil or parchment paper. Ensure they are securely placed and do not block the air vents. Avoid covering the entire basket as this can obstruct airflow and affect cooking performance.
2. **Do I Need to Preheat the Air Fryer?**
   - o **Answer**: Preheating is recommended for optimal cooking results. It helps achieve the desired temperature before you start cooking, ensuring even and consistent results.
3. **How Much Oil Should I Use?**
   - o **Answer**: One of the benefits of air frying is the reduced need for oil. A light spray or a teaspoon of oil is usually sufficient. Using too much oil can lead to excess smoking and affect the crispiness of the food.
4. **Can I Cook Frozen Foods Directly in the Air Fryer?**
   - o **Answer**: Yes, you can cook frozen foods directly in the air fryer. Adjust the cooking time and temperature as needed. Preheating can help achieve better results.
5. **How Do I Clean the Air Fryer?**
   - o **Answer**: Ensure the air fryer is unplugged and completely cool before cleaning. The basket and crisper plate are typically dishwasher safe. For manual cleaning, use warm, soapy water and a non-abrasive sponge. Wipe the interior and exterior with a damp cloth.
6. **Why Is My Food Sticking to the Basket?**
   - o **Answer**: Ensure the basket is properly cleaned and dried before use. Lightly coat the basket and food with oil to prevent sticking. Avoid using cooking sprays that contain propellants, as they can damage the nonstick coating.
7. **Can I Open the Basket During Cooking?**
   - o **Answer**: Yes, you can open the basket during cooking to shake or flip the food. The air fryer will pause when the basket is removed and resume cooking when it's replaced.
8. **What Foods Are Best Suited for Air Frying?**
   - o **Answer**: Air frying is versatile and works well with a variety of foods, including vegetables, meats, seafood, and frozen snacks. It's particularly effective for foods that benefit from a crispy texture.

By addressing common issues and understanding the answers to frequently asked questions, you'll be better equipped to use your Ninja Air Fryer Pro effectively and troubleshoot any problems that may arise. Enjoy hassle-free cooking with this versatile and powerful kitchen appliance.

AIRFRYER BREAKFAST RECIPES

Air Fryer French Toast Sticks

These Air Fryer French Toast Sticks offer a crispy exterior and a soft, custardy center, perfect for a quick and delicious breakfast. Made with minimal oil, they're a healthier alternative to traditional French toast.

Tools needed:

Ninja Air Fryer Pro
Shallow bowl
Whisk
Bread knife
Air fryer basket

2. In a shallow bowl, whisk together eggs, milk, sugar, vanilla extract, and cinnamon.
3. Cut the bread into sticks, approximately 1-inch wide.
4. Dip each bread stick into the egg mixture, ensuring it's well coated.
5. Place the coated sticks in the air fryer basket in a single layer. Cook for 8-10 minutes, flipping halfway through, until golden brown and crispy.
6. Remove from the air fryer and dust with powdered sugar. Serve with maple syrup.

Ingredients:

- 4 slices of thick bread (e.g., brioche or challah)
- 2 large eggs
- 1/2 cup milk
- 1/4 cup granulated sugar
- 1 teaspoon vanilla extract
- 1/2 teaspoon ground cinnamon
- Powdered sugar (for serving)
- Maple syrup (for serving)

Direction:

1. Preheat the air fryer to 375°F (190°C).

Servings: 4 | **Prep time:** 10 minutes | **Cooking time:** 8-10 minutes

Nutritional info (per serving):
Calories: 180
Protein: 6g
Fat: 6g
Carbohydrates: 25g
Sugar: 12g

Quick tips:

- Use thicker slices of bread for a better texture.
- If cooking multiple batches, keep the French toast sticks warm in the oven while preparing the rest.

Crispy Breakfast Hash Browns made in the air fryer are a perfect start to your day. They offer a golden, crispy exterior and tender interior without the excess oil of traditional frying.

Tools needed:

Ninja Air Fryer Pro
Box grater or food processor
Cheesecloth or paper towels
Mixing bowl
Air fryer basket

Ingredients:

- 2 large russet potatoes, peeled and grated
- 1 small onion, finely chopped
- 1 large egg
- 1/4 cup all-purpose flour
- 1 teaspoon garlic powder
- 1/2 teaspoon paprika
- Salt and pepper to taste
- 1 tablespoon olive oil

Direction:

1. Preheat the air fryer to 400°F (200°C).
2. Place the grated potatoes in a cheesecloth or paper towel and squeeze out as much moisture as possible.
3. In a mixing bowl, combine grated potatoes, chopped onion, egg, flour, garlic powder, paprika, salt, and pepper.
4. Form the mixture into small patties.
5. Brush each patty lightly with olive oil and place them in the air fryer basket in a single layer.
6. Cook for 12-15 minutes, flipping halfway through, until golden and crispy.

Servings: 4 | **Prep time:** 15 minutes | **Cooking time:** 12-15 minutes

Nutritional info (per serving):
Calories: 150
Protein: 3g
Fat: 5g
Carbohydrates: 22g
Sugar: 2g

Quick tips:

- Ensure the potatoes are thoroughly dried to achieve maximum crispiness.
- Cook in batches if necessary to avoid overcrowding the air fryer.

Air Fried Avocado Toast combines the creamy texture of avocado with a perfectly crispy toast, making it a quick and healthy breakfast option or snack.

Tools needed:

Ninja Air Fryer Pro
Fork
Bread knife
Mixing bowl
Air fryer basket

Ingredients:

- 2 slices of whole-grain bread
- 1 ripe avocado
- 1 tablespoon lemon juice
- Salt and pepper to taste
- Optional toppings: cherry tomatoes, radishes, or a poached egg

Direction:

1. Preheat the air fryer to 370°F (188°C).

2. Toast the bread slices in the air fryer for 3-5 minutes until crispy.
3. While the bread is toasting, mash the avocado in a mixing bowl with lemon juice, salt, and pepper.
4. Spread the mashed avocado evenly over the toasted bread.
5. Add optional toppings if desired. Serve immediately.

Servings: 2 | **Prep time:** 5 minutes | **Cooking time:** 3-5 minutes

Nutritional info (per serving):
Calories: 230
Protein: 5g
Fat: 12g
Carbohydrates: 28g
Sugar: 2g

Quick tips:

- Choose ripe avocados for the best texture and flavor.
- Experiment with different toppings to customize your avocado toast.

Breakfast Egg Muffins are a convenient and nutritious option for a busy morning. These savory muffins are packed with protein and can be customized with your favorite vegetables and meats.

Tools needed:

- Ninja Air Fryer Pro
- Muffin tin (oven-safe or silicone)
- Mixing bowl
- Whisk
- Air fryer basket

Ingredients:

- 6 large eggs
- 1/2 cup milk
- 1/2 cup shredded cheese (cheddar, mozzarella, or your choice)
- 1/2 cup diced bell peppers
- 1/2 cup diced onions
- 1/2 cup cooked and crumbled bacon or sausage (optional)
- Salt and pepper to taste
- Cooking spray or oil for greasing

Direction:

1. Preheat the air fryer to 350°F (175°C).
2. In a mixing bowl, whisk together eggs and milk. Stir in cheese, bell peppers, onions, bacon or sausage (if using), salt, and pepper.
3. Grease the muffin tin with cooking spray or oil.
4. Pour the egg mixture evenly into the muffin cups.
5. Place the muffin tin in the air fryer basket and cook for 12-15 minutes, or until the egg muffins are set and golden brown on top.
6. Let cool slightly before removing from the tin.

Servings: 6 | **Prep time:** 10 minutes | **Cooking time:** 12-15 minutes

Nutritional info (per serving):
Calories: 150
Protein: 10g
Fat: 11g
Carbohydrates: 2g
Sugar: 1g

Quick tips:

- Feel free to add your favorite vegetables or meats to the egg mixture for added flavor.
- Use silicone muffin cups for easy removal and clean-up.

Air Fryer Cinnamon Rolls

Air Fryer Cinnamon Rolls are a quick and easy way to enjoy a warm, gooey breakfast treat without the need for an oven. They offer a perfectly crispy exterior and soft, cinnamon-sugar center.

Tools needed:

- Ninja Air Fryer Pro
- Rolling pin
- Air fryer basket
- Small mixing bowl

Ingredients:

- 1 can refrigerated cinnamon roll dough (with icing included)
- 1 tablespoon melted butter (for brushing)
- Optional: extra cinnamon sugar for sprinkling

Direction:

1. Preheat the air fryer to 350°F (175°C).
2. Open the can of cinnamon roll dough and separate the rolls.
3. Brush each roll with melted butter and sprinkle with extra cinnamon sugar if desired.
4. Place the rolls in the air fryer basket, making sure they are not touching each other.
5. Cook for 8-10 minutes, or until the rolls are golden brown and cooked through.
6. Drizzle the included icing over the warm rolls before serving.

Servings: 8 rolls | **Prep time:** 5 minutes | **Cooking time:** 8-10 minutes

Nutritional info (per roll):
Calories: 200
Protein: 2g
Fat: 9g
Carbohydrates: 28g
Sugar: 15g

Quick tips:

- For even cooking, avoid overcrowding the basket; cook in batches if necessary.
- Serve immediately for the best texture and flavor.

Banana Bread Bites are a delightful, bite-sized treat that offers the classic flavor of banana bread in a more convenient form. Perfect for snacking or breakfast, these bites are moist and sweet.

Tools needed:

- Ninja Air Fryer Pro
- Mini muffin tin or silicone molds
- Mixing bowl
- Whisk

Ingredients:

- 1 cup mashed ripe bananas (about 2 large bananas)
- 1/2 cup granulated sugar
- 1/4 cup melted butter
- 1 large egg
- 1 teaspoon vanilla extract
- 1 teaspoon baking powder
- 1/4 teaspoon salt
- 1 cup all-purpose flour
- Optional: 1/4 cup chopped nuts or chocolate chips

Direction:

1. Preheat the air fryer to 350°F (175°C).
2. In a mixing bowl, combine mashed bananas, sugar, melted butter, egg, and vanilla extract.
3. Stir in baking powder, salt, and flour until just combined. Fold in nuts or chocolate chips if using.
4. Grease the mini muffin tin or silicone molds.
5. Spoon the batter into the molds, filling each about 3/4 full.
6. Place the muffin tin in the air fryer basket and cook for 8-10 minutes, or until a toothpick inserted into the center comes out clean.
7. Allow the banana bread bites to cool before removing from the molds.

Servings: 24 bites | **Prep time:** 10 minutes | **Cooking time:** 8-10 minutes

Nutritional info (per bite): Calories: 80, Protein: 1g, Fat: 4g, Carbohydrates: 10g, Sugar: 6g

Quick tips:

- Use very ripe bananas for the best flavor and sweetness.
- For even cooking, avoid overcrowding the mini muffin tin; cook in batches if necessary.

Sweet Potato Breakfast Fries

Sweet Potato Breakfast Fries are a nutritious and delicious alternative to traditional breakfast potatoes. Crisp on the outside and tender on the inside, these fries make a perfect addition to your morning meal or a tasty snack.

Tools needed:

- Ninja Air Fryer Pro
- Knife
- Cutting board
- Mixing bowl
- Air fryer basket

Ingredients:

- 2 large sweet potatoes, peeled and cut into fry shapes
- 1 tablespoon olive oil
- 1 teaspoon paprika
- 1/2 teaspoon garlic powder
- 1/2 teaspoon onion powder
- Salt and pepper to taste

Direction:

1. Preheat the air fryer to 400°F (200°C).
2. In a mixing bowl, toss the sweet potato fries with olive oil, paprika, garlic powder, onion powder, salt, and pepper.
3. Arrange the fries in a single layer in the air fryer basket. Cook in batches if necessary.
4. Air fry for 15-20 minutes, shaking the basket halfway through, until the fries are crispy and golden brown.
5. Serve immediately.

Servings: 4 | **Prep time:** 10 minutes | **Cooking time:** 15-20 minutes

Nutritional info (per serving):
Calories: 150
Protein: 2g
Fat: 6g
Carbohydrates: 23g
Sugar: 6g

Quick tips:

- For extra crispiness, soak the cut sweet potatoes in water for 30 minutes before cooking, then pat dry thoroughly.
- Adjust seasoning to taste and experiment with different spices.

Air Fried Oatmeal Cups

Air Fried Oatmeal Cups are a convenient and customizable breakfast option. Packed with oats and fruit, these cups are both hearty and healthy, perfect for busy mornings.

Tools needed:

- Ninja Air Fryer Pro
- Muffin tin (oven-safe or silicone)
- Mixing bowl
- Whisk

Ingredients:

- 1 1/2 cups rolled oats
- 1 cup milk (any type)
- 1/2 cup mashed banana (about 1 ripe banana)
- 1/4 cup honey or maple syrup
- 1/2 teaspoon vanilla extract
- 1/2 teaspoon ground cinnamon
- 1/2 cup diced apples or berries (fresh or frozen)
- Optional: nuts or seeds for topping

Direction:

1. Preheat the air fryer to 350°F (175°C).
2. In a mixing bowl, combine oats, milk, mashed banana, honey or maple syrup, vanilla extract, and cinnamon. Stir in diced apples or berries.
3. Grease the muffin tin with cooking spray or oil.
4. Spoon the oatmeal mixture into the muffin cups, filling each about 3/4 full. Top with nuts or seeds if desired.
5. Place the muffin tin in the air fryer basket and cook for 10-12 minutes, or until the tops are golden brown and the oatmeal is set.
6. Let cool slightly before removing from the tin.

Servings: 6 | **Prep time:** 10 minutes | **Cooking time:** 10-12 minutes

Nutritional info (per cup):
Calories: 180
Protein: 5g
Fat: 4g
Carbohydrates: 32g
Sugar: 12g

Quick tips:

- Use silicone muffin cups for easy removal and clean-up.
- Customize with your favorite fruits and nuts for added flavor and texture.

Apple Cinnamon Breakfast Donuts

Apple Cinnamon Breakfast Donuts are a delightful treat that combines the flavors of fresh apples and warm cinnamon in a baked donut form. Made in the air fryer, these donuts are a healthier alternative to traditional fried donuts.

Tools needed:

- Ninja Air Fryer Pro
- Donut pan (oven-safe or silicone)
- Mixing bowl
- Whisk

Ingredients:

- 1 cup all-purpose flour
- 1/2 cup granulated sugar
- 1/2 teaspoon baking powder
- 1/2 teaspoon ground cinnamon
- 1/4 teaspoon salt
- 1/2 cup milk
- 1/4 cup applesauce
- 1 large egg
- 1/2 cup finely chopped apple (peeled)

Direction:

1. Preheat the air fryer to 360°F (180°C).
2. In a mixing bowl, whisk together flour, sugar, baking powder, cinnamon, and salt.
3. In another bowl, mix milk, applesauce, and egg. Stir into the dry ingredients until just combined. Fold in chopped apple.
4. Grease the donut pan with cooking spray or oil.
5. Spoon the batter into the donut pan, filling each mold about 3/4 full.
6. Place the pan in the air fryer basket and cook for 8-10 minutes, or until a toothpick inserted into the center comes out clean.
7. Allow the donuts to cool slightly before removing from the pan.

Servings: 6 | **Prep time:** 10 minutes | **Cooking time:** 8-10 minutes

Nutritional info (per donut): Calories: 160, Protein: 3g, Fat: 4g, Carbohydrates: 28g, Sugar: 12g

Quick tips:

- For extra flavor, sprinkle with a mixture of sugar and cinnamon after cooking.
- Ensure the donut pan is well greased to prevent sticking.

Breakfast Burrito Pockets are a fun and portable breakfast option filled with savory ingredients. Made in the air fryer, these pockets offer a crispy exterior and a flavorful, satisfying filling.

Tools needed:

- Ninja Air Fryer Pro
- Rolling pin
- Knife
- Mixing bowl
- Air fryer basket

Ingredients:

- 4 large flour tortillas
- 1 cup scrambled eggs
- 1/2 cup cooked and crumbled breakfast sausage or bacon
- 1/2 cup shredded cheese (cheddar or mozzarella)
- 1/4 cup diced bell peppers
- 1/4 cup diced onions
- 1 tablespoon olive oil
- Salt and pepper to taste

Direction:

1. Preheat the air fryer to 350°F (175°C).
2. In a mixing bowl, combine scrambled eggs, sausage or bacon, cheese, bell peppers, onions, salt, and pepper.
3. Place one tortilla on a flat surface and spoon about 1/4 of the filling mixture into the center.
4. Fold the sides of the tortilla over the filling and roll it up to form a pocket. Secure with toothpicks if needed.
5. Brush the outside of each pocket lightly with olive oil.
6. Place the burrito pockets in the air fryer basket, making sure they are not touching.
7. Cook for 8-10 minutes, flipping halfway through, until golden brown and crispy.
8. Remove from the air fryer and let cool slightly before serving.

Servings: 4 | **Prep time:** 10 minutes | **Cooking time:** 8-10 minutes

Nutritional info (per pocket): Calories: 250, Protein: 12g, Fat: 14g, Carbohydrates: 20g, Sugar: 2g

Quick tips:

- Customize with your favorite fillings, such as vegetables, different cheeses, or additional proteins.
- Use toothpicks to secure the pockets if they're having trouble holding their shape.

AIRFRYER POULTRY RECIPES

Air Fryer Cilantro Lime Chicken

Air Fryer Cilantro Lime Chicken is a zesty and flavorful dish that is quick to prepare. The combination of lime and cilantro adds a fresh twist to the tender chicken breasts.

Tools needed:

- Ninja Air Fryer Pro
- Mixing bowl
- Air fryer basket

Ingredients:

- 4 boneless, skinless chicken breasts
- 2 tablespoons olive oil
- Juice of 2 limes
- 1/4 cup chopped fresh cilantro
- 2 cloves garlic, minced
- 1 teaspoon ground cumin
- 1/2 teaspoon paprika
- Salt and pepper to taste

Direction:

1. Preheat the air fryer to 375°F (190°C).
2. In a mixing bowl, combine olive oil, lime juice, cilantro, garlic, cumin, paprika, salt, and pepper.
3. Coat the chicken breasts evenly with the marinade. Let marinate for at least 15 minutes.
4. Place the chicken breasts in the air fryer basket in a single layer.
5. Cook for 15-18 minutes, flipping halfway through, until the chicken is cooked through and has an internal temperature of 165°F (74°C).
6. Let the chicken rest for a few minutes before slicing and serving.

Servings: 4 | **Prep time:** 15 minutes | **Cooking time:** 15-18 minutes

Nutritional info (per serving):
Calories: 220
Protein: 30g
Fat: 10g
Carbohydrates: 2g
Sugar: 1g

Quick tips:

- For added flavor, try garnishing with extra cilantro and lime wedges before serving.
- Ensure the chicken breasts are of similar thickness for even cooking.

Gochujang Chicken Wings offer a spicy, tangy flavor with a touch of sweetness. This Korean-inspired recipe is perfect for a flavorful appetizer or main dish.

Tools needed:

- Ninja Air Fryer Pro
- Mixing bowl
- Air fryer basket

Ingredients:

- 2 pounds chicken wings
- 1/4 cup gochujang (Korean chili paste)
- 2 tablespoons soy sauce
- 2 tablespoons honey
- 1 tablespoon rice vinegar
- 1 tablespoon sesame oil
- 2 cloves garlic, minced
- 1 teaspoon grated ginger
- Sesame seeds and chopped green onions for garnish (optional)

Direction:

1. Preheat the air fryer to 380°F (193°C).
2. In a mixing bowl, whisk together gochujang, soy sauce, honey, rice vinegar, sesame oil, garlic, and ginger.
3. Toss the chicken wings in the sauce mixture until well coated.
4. Place the wings in the air fryer basket in a single layer. Cook in batches if necessary.
5. Air fry for 20-25 minutes, flipping halfway through, until the wings are crispy and cooked through.
6. Garnish with sesame seeds and chopped green onions if desired before serving.

Servings: 4 | **Prep time:** 15 minutes | **Cooking time:** 20-25 minutes

Nutritional info (per serving, 6 wings):
Calories: 300
Protein: 20g
Fat: 20g
Carbohydrates: 12g
Sugar: 8g

Quick tips:

- For extra crispiness, pat the wings dry with paper towels before coating them in the sauce.
- Adjust the level of gochujang to control the spiciness of the wings.

Chicken Tikka Masala

Chicken Tikka Masala is a rich and creamy Indian dish known for its spicy and aromatic flavor. Using the air fryer, you can achieve tender, flavorful chicken with a fraction of the traditional cooking time.

Tools needed:

Ninja Air Fryer Pro
Mixing bowls
Air fryer basket
Small saucepan

Ingredients:

For the Chicken Marinade:

1 pound boneless, skinless chicken thighs, cut into chunks
1 cup plain yogurt
2 tablespoons lemon juice
1 tablespoon ground cumin
1 tablespoon ground coriander
1 teaspoon ground turmeric
1 teaspoon garam masala
1 teaspoon paprika
2 cloves garlic, minced
1 tablespoon grated ginger
Salt to taste

For the Sauce:

2 tablespoons olive oil
1 large onion, finely chopped
2 cloves garlic, minced
1 tablespoon grated ginger
1 can (14.5 ounces) crushed tomatoes
1 cup heavy cream
1 tablespoon garam masala
1 teaspoon ground cumin
1 teaspoon paprika
1/2 teaspoon ground turmeric
Salt and pepper to taste

Fresh cilantro for garnish (optional)

Directions:

Mix all marinade ingredients in a bowl, add chicken, coat thoroughly, and marinate in the refrigerator for at least 1 hour or overnight.
Preheat air fryer to 375°F (190°C).
Remove chicken from marinade, arrange in a single layer in the air fryer basket, and air fry for 12-15 minutes, turning halfway, until cooked through and internal temperature reaches 165°F (74°C).
For the sauce, heat olive oil in a saucepan over medium heat, sauté onions until translucent, then add garlic and ginger and cook for 2 minutes.
Stir in crushed tomatoes, cream, garam masala, cumin, paprika, turmeric, salt, and pepper, and simmer for 10 minutes, stirring occasionally.
Add cooked chicken to the sauce, stir to coat, and simmer for another 5 minutes. Garnish with fresh cilantro if desired and serve with rice or naan.

Servings: 4 | **Prep time:** 15 minutes (plus marinating time) | **Cooking time:** 20 minutes

Nutritional info (per serving): Calories: 350, Protein: 30g, Fat: 22g, Carbohydrates: 12g, Sugar: 8g

Quick tips:

- Adjust the level of spices in the marinade and sauce to suit your taste.
- Serve with steamed rice or naan bread to complete the meal.

Chicken Enchiladas

Chicken Enchiladas are a classic Mexican dish that combines tender chicken with spicy enchilada sauce and melted cheese. This recipe uses the air fryer for a quicker, yet equally delicious version.

Tools needed:

Ninja Air Fryer Pro
Mixing bowls
Air fryer basket
Baking dish

Ingredients:

2 cups cooked, shredded chicken (about 2 chicken breasts)
1 cup shredded cheese (cheddar or Monterey Jack)
1 cup enchilada sauce
8 small flour or corn tortillas
1/2 cup finely chopped onions
1/2 cup chopped bell peppers
1 tablespoon olive oil
1 teaspoon ground cumin
1/2 teaspoon chili powder
Salt and pepper to taste
Fresh cilantro for garnish (optional)

Direction:

1. Preheat the air fryer to 350°F (175°C).
2. In a mixing bowl, combine shredded chicken, half of the cheese, onions, bell peppers, cumin, chili powder, salt, and pepper.
3. Spread a small amount of enchilada sauce on the bottom of the baking dish or air fryer pan.
4. Fill each tortilla with the chicken mixture, roll up, and place seam-side down in the dish or pan.
5. Pour the remaining enchilada sauce over the rolled tortillas and sprinkle with the remaining cheese.
6. Place the baking dish or pan in the air fryer basket and cook for 12-15 minutes, or until the cheese is melted and bubbly.
7. Garnish with fresh cilantro if desired and serve with sour cream or salsa.

Servings: 4 | **Prep time:** 15 minutes | **Cooking time:** 12-15 minutes

Nutritional info (per serving, 2 enchiladas): Calories: 350, Protein: 25g, Fat: 15g, Carbohydrates: 30g, Sugar: 5g

Lemon Herb Air Fryer Chicken Breast is a simple yet flavorful dish featuring tender chicken breasts marinated in a zesty lemon and herb mixture. Perfect for a quick weeknight dinner or meal prep.

Tools needed:

- Ninja Air Fryer Pro
- Mixing bowl
- Air fryer basket

Ingredients:

- 4 boneless, skinless chicken breasts
- 2 tablespoons olive oil
- Juice and zest of 1 lemon
- 2 cloves garlic, minced
- 1 tablespoon chopped fresh rosemary (or 1 teaspoon dried)
- 1 tablespoon chopped fresh thyme (or 1 teaspoon dried)
- Salt and pepper to taste

Direction:

1. Preheat the air fryer to 375°F (190°C).
2. In a mixing bowl, whisk together olive oil, lemon juice, lemon zest, garlic, rosemary, thyme, salt, and pepper.
3. Coat the chicken breasts with the marinade and let them sit for at least 15 minutes.
4. Place the chicken breasts in the air fryer basket in a single layer.
5. Air fry for 15-18 minutes, flipping halfway through, until the chicken is cooked through and has an internal temperature of 165°F (74°C).
6. Let the chicken rest for a few minutes before slicing and serving.

Servings: 4 | **Prep time:** 15 minutes | **Cooking time:** 15-18 minutes

Nutritional info (per serving):
Calories: 220
Protein: 30g
Fat: 10g
Carbohydrates: 2g
Sugar: 1g

Quick tips:

- For a more intense flavor, let the chicken marinate for several hours or overnight.
- Serve with a side of vegetables or a fresh salad for a complete meal.

Honey Garlic Chicken Thighs are a savory and sweet dish with a sticky glaze that's perfect for a delicious dinner. The air fryer gives these thighs a crispy exterior while keeping the inside juicy and tender.

Tools needed:

- Ninja Air Fryer Pro
- Mixing bowls
- Air fryer basket
- Small saucepan

Ingredients:

- 4 bone-in, skinless chicken thighs
- 1/4 cup honey
- 3 tablespoons soy sauce
- 3 cloves garlic, minced
- 1 tablespoon olive oil
- 1 tablespoon rice vinegar
- 1 teaspoon ground ginger
- 1/2 teaspoon red pepper flakes (optional for heat)
- Salt and pepper to taste

Direction:

1. Preheat the air fryer to 380°F (193°C).
2. In a small saucepan, combine honey, soy sauce, garlic, olive oil, rice vinegar, ginger, and red pepper flakes. Heat over medium heat, stirring occasionally, until the sauce thickens slightly (about 5 minutes). Set aside.
3. Season the chicken thighs with salt and pepper. Brush with a little bit of the honey garlic sauce.
4. Place the chicken thighs in the air fryer basket in a single layer.
5. Air fry for 20-25 minutes, flipping halfway through, until the chicken reaches an internal temperature of 165°F (74°C) and the skin is crispy.
6. Brush the chicken with the remaining honey garlic sauce before serving.

Servings: 4 | **Prep time:** 10 minutes | **Cooking time:** 20-25 minutes

Nutritional info (per serving): Calories: 270, Protein: 22g, Fat: 18g, Carbohydrates: 14g, Sugar: 13g

Quick tips:

- For extra crispiness, pat the chicken thighs dry before seasoning.
- If you like more sauce, double the ingredients for the glaze and serve extra on the side.

Air Fried Buffalo Drumsticks

Air Fried Buffalo Drumsticks bring the heat with spicy buffalo sauce while being crispy on the outside and juicy on the inside. This recipe is perfect for game day or a satisfying snack.

Tools needed:

- Ninja Air Fryer Pro
- Mixing bowls
- Air fryer basket

Ingredients:

- 8 chicken drumsticks
- 1/4 cup olive oil
- 1 cup buffalo sauce
- 1 teaspoon garlic powder
- 1 teaspoon onion powder
- Salt and pepper to taste
- Celery sticks and ranch dressing for serving (optional)

Direction:

1. Preheat the air fryer to 400°F (200°C).
2. In a mixing bowl, toss the drumsticks with olive oil, garlic powder, onion powder, salt, and pepper.
3. Place the drumsticks in the air fryer basket in a single layer.
4. Air fry for 25-30 minutes, flipping halfway through, until the drumsticks are crispy and cooked through (internal temperature of 165°F or 74°C).
5. Toss the cooked drumsticks in buffalo sauce and return to the air fryer for an additional 2-3 minutes to set the sauce.
6. Serve with celery sticks and ranch dressing if desired.

Servings: 4 | **Prep time:** 10 minutes | **Cooking time:** 25-30 minutes

Nutritional info (per drumstick):
Calories: 250
Protein: 20g
Fat: 18g
Carbohydrates: 2g
Sugar: 0g

Quick tips:

- For a milder version, use a milder buffalo sauce or adjust the amount to taste.
- To make the drumsticks extra crispy, pat them dry before seasoning and avoid overcrowding the air fryer basket.

Parmesan Crusted Chicken offers a deliciously crunchy coating with a rich, cheesy flavor. The air fryer ensures a crispy crust without the need for excessive oil, making this a healthier alternative to traditional fried chicken.

Tools needed:

- Ninja Air Fryer Pro
- Mixing bowls
- Air fryer basket
- Cooking spray

Ingredients:

- 4 boneless, skinless chicken breasts
- 1/2 cup grated Parmesan cheese
- 1/2 cup panko breadcrumbs
- 1 teaspoon dried Italian seasoning
- 1/2 teaspoon garlic powder
- 1/2 teaspoon onion powder
- 1/2 teaspoon paprika
- 2 large eggs, beaten
- Salt and pepper to taste
- Cooking spray

Direction:

1. Preheat the air fryer to 375°F (190°C).
2. In a shallow bowl, mix Parmesan cheese, panko breadcrumbs, Italian seasoning, garlic powder, onion powder, paprika, salt, and pepper.
3. Dip each chicken breast in the beaten eggs, then coat with the Parmesan mixture, pressing down to adhere well.
4. Spray the air fryer basket with cooking spray and place the coated chicken breasts in the basket.
5. Air fry for 15-18 minutes, flipping halfway through, until the chicken is golden brown and has an internal temperature of 165°F (74°C).
6. Serve with a side salad or your favorite dipping sauce.

Servings: 4 | **Prep time:** 10 minutes | **Cooking time:** 15-18 minutes

Nutritional info (per serving): Calories: 280, Protein: 32g, Fat: 14g, Carbohydrates: 10g, Sugar: 2g

Quick tips:

- For a more flavorful crust, add additional herbs and spices to the Parmesan mixture.
- Ensure the chicken is evenly coated for a consistent, crispy texture.

Teriyaki Chicken Bites

Teriyaki Chicken Bites are flavorful and tender morsels of chicken coated in a sweet and savory teriyaki sauce. Air frying gives them a deliciously crispy exterior with a juicy inside.

Tools needed:

Ninja Air Fryer Pro
Mixing bowls
Air fryer basket
Small saucepan

Ingredients:

For the Chicken:

- 1 pound boneless, skinless chicken breasts, cut into bite-sized pieces
- 2 tablespoons olive oil
- Salt and pepper to taste

For the Teriyaki Sauce:

- 1/4 cup soy sauce
- 1/4 cup honey
- 2 tablespoons rice vinegar
- 1 tablespoon cornstarch mixed with 1 tablespoon water (for thickening)
- 2 cloves garlic, minced
- 1 teaspoon grated ginger
- 1 teaspoon sesame seeds (optional for garnish)
- Sliced green onions (optional for garnish)

Direction:

1. Preheat the air fryer to 380°F (193°C).

2. Toss the chicken pieces with olive oil, salt, and pepper.
3. In a small saucepan, combine soy sauce, honey, rice vinegar, garlic, and ginger. Bring to a simmer over medium heat.
4. Stir in the cornstarch mixture and continue to simmer until the sauce thickens, about 3-4 minutes. Remove from heat and set aside.
5. Place the chicken pieces in the air fryer basket in a single layer.
6. Air fry for 10-12 minutes, shaking the basket halfway through, until the chicken is cooked through and crispy.
7. Toss the cooked chicken in the teriyaki sauce and return to the air fryer for an additional 2-3 minutes to set the sauce.
8. Garnish with sesame seeds and green onions if desired before serving.

Servings: 4 | **Prep time:** 15 minutes | **Cooking time:** 12-15 minutes

Nutritional info (per serving):
Calories: 290
Protein: 27g
Fat: 10g
Carbohydrates: 20g
Sugar: 16g

Quick tips:

- For extra flavor, marinate the chicken in a little bit of teriyaki sauce for 30 minutes before air frying.
- Serve with steamed rice and vegetables for a complete meal.

Spicy Sriracha Chicken Nuggets offer a crispy coating with a fiery kick, perfect for those who love a bit of heat. These nuggets are quick to make in the air fryer and are great as a snack or appetizer.

Tools needed:

- Ninja Air Fryer Pro
- Mixing bowls
- Air fryer basket
- Cooking spray

Ingredients:

- 1 pound boneless, skinless chicken breasts, cut into nugget-sized pieces
- 1/2 cup all-purpose flour
- 1/2 cup panko breadcrumbs
- 1/4 cup grated Parmesan cheese
- 1/4 cup Sriracha sauce
- 2 large eggs, beaten
- 1 teaspoon garlic powder
- 1 teaspoon onion powder
- Salt and pepper to taste
- Cooking spray

Direction:

1. Preheat the air fryer to 400°F (200°C).
2. In a bowl, combine flour, garlic powder, onion powder, salt, and pepper.
3. In another bowl, mix the panko breadcrumbs and Parmesan cheese.
4. Coat each chicken nugget first in the flour mixture, then dip in beaten eggs, and finally coat with the breadcrumb mixture.
5. Place the coated chicken nuggets in the air fryer basket in a single layer and spray lightly with cooking spray.
6. Air fry for 10-12 minutes, flipping halfway through, until the nuggets are golden brown and crispy.
7. Toss the cooked nuggets in Sriracha sauce and serve hot.

Servings: 4 | **Prep time:** 15 minutes | **Cooking time:** 10-12 minutes

Nutritional info (per serving, 4 nuggets): Calories: 320, Fat: 15g, Carbohydrates: 25g, Sugar: 3g

Quick tips:

- Adjust the amount of Sriracha sauce to control the level of spiciness.
- For extra crunch, add a bit more Parmesan to the breadcrumb mixture.

AIRFRYER BEEF RECIPES

Beef Stroganoff

Beef Stroganoff is a classic, creamy dish featuring tender strips of beef in a savory mushroom sauce. Using the air fryer speeds up the cooking process while still delivering the rich flavors of this comforting dish.

Tools needed:

Ninja Air Fryer Pro
Mixing bowls
Air fryer basket
Large skillet or saucepan

Ingredients:

- 1 pound beef sirloin, cut into thin strips
- 1 cup sliced mushrooms
- 1 small onion, finely chopped
- 2 cloves garlic, minced
- 1 cup beef broth
- 1 cup sour cream
- 1 tablespoon flour
- 1 tablespoon olive oil
- 1 teaspoon paprika
- Salt and pepper to taste
- Fresh parsley for garnish (optional)

Direction:

1. Preheat the air fryer to 400°F (200°C).
2. Toss the beef strips with paprika, salt, and pepper.
3. Place the beef strips in the air fryer basket in a single layer and cook for 8-10 minutes, shaking halfway through, until browned and cooked to your desired doneness.
4. While the beef is cooking, heat olive oil in a skillet over medium heat. Sauté onions, garlic, and mushrooms until soft.
5. Stir in the flour and cook for 1 minute. Gradually add beef broth, stirring constantly, until the mixture thickens.
6. Reduce heat and stir in the sour cream. Cook for an additional 2-3 minutes until well combined and heated through.
7. Add the cooked beef strips to the sauce and stir to combine. Garnish with fresh parsley if desired before serving.

Servings: 4 | **Prep time:** 10 minutes | **Cooking time:** 8-10 minutes (plus sauce preparation)

Nutritional info (per serving): Calories: 350, Protein: 25g, Fat: 20g, Carbohydrates: 15g, Sugar: 6g

Quick tips:

- Serve over egg noodles or rice to soak up the delicious sauce.
- For a richer flavor, use a combination of beef broth and a splash of red wine.

Beef Taquitos

Beef Taquitos are crispy, rolled tortillas filled with seasoned ground beef. The air fryer gives them a perfectly crispy exterior while keeping the beef flavorful and tender.

Tools needed:

Ninja Air Fryer Pro
Mixing bowls
Air fryer basket
Large skillet
Toothpicks or cooking twine

Ingredients:

- 1 pound ground beef
- 1 small onion, finely chopped
- 2 cloves garlic, minced
- 1 teaspoon chili powder
- 1/2 teaspoon cumin
- 1/2 teaspoon paprika
- 1/4 teaspoon salt
- 1/4 teaspoon black pepper
- 8 small flour or corn tortillas
- 1 cup shredded cheddar cheese
- Cooking spray
- Salsa and sour cream for serving (optional)

Direction:

1. Preheat the air fryer to 400°F (200°C).
2. In a large skillet over medium heat, cook the ground beef, onion, and garlic until the beef is browned and the onion is translucent. Drain any excess fat.
3. Stir in chili powder, cumin, paprika, salt, and pepper. Cook for another 2 minutes. Remove from heat.
4. Place a small amount of beef mixture and shredded cheese in the center of each tortilla. Roll tightly and secure with toothpicks or cooking twine.
5. Spray the air fryer basket with cooking spray and place the taquitos in a single layer.
6. Air fry for 8-10 minutes, turning halfway through, until the taquitos are golden brown and crispy.
7. Serve with salsa and sour cream if desired.

Servings: 4 | **Prep time:** 15 minutes | **Cooking time:** 8-10 minutes

Nutritional info (per serving, 2 taquitos): Calories: 320, Protein: 20g, Fat: 15g, Carbohydrates: 30g, Sugar: 2g
Quick tips:

- For extra flavor, add chopped cilantro or a squeeze of lime juice to the beef mixture.

Crispy Air Fryer Beef Tacos are packed with seasoned ground beef and topped with fresh ingredients. The air fryer creates a crunchy shell that perfectly complements the juicy beef filling.

Tools needed:

- Ninja Air Fryer Pro
- Mixing bowls
- Air fryer basket

Ingredients:

- 1 pound ground beef
- 1 small onion, finely chopped
- 2 cloves garlic, minced
- 1 packet taco seasoning
- 1/2 cup water
- 8 small taco shells (corn or flour)
- 1 cup shredded lettuce
- 1/2 cup diced tomatoes
- 1/2 cup shredded cheese
- Sour cream and salsa for serving (optional)

Direction:

1. Preheat the air fryer to 400°F (200°C).
2. In a skillet over medium heat, cook the ground beef, onion, and garlic until the beef is browned and the onion is translucent. Drain any excess fat.
3. Stir in taco seasoning and water, simmering for 5 minutes until the mixture thickens.
4. Arrange the taco shells in the air fryer basket. Air fry for 2-3 minutes to crisp up the shells.
5. Fill the taco shells with the beef mixture and top with shredded lettuce, diced tomatoes, and cheese.
6. Serve with sour cream and salsa if desired.

Servings: 4 | **Prep time:** 10 minutes | **Cooking time:** 5-7 minutes

Nutritional info (per serving, 2 tacos): Calories: 310, Protein: 22g, Fat: 16g, Carbohydrates: 22g, Sugar: 3g

Quick tips:

- To make the tacos extra crispy, air fry the filled tacos for an additional 2-3 minutes.
- Customize toppings based on your preference, such as adding sliced jalapeños or chopped cilantro.

Air Fried Steak Bites

Air Fried Steak Bites are tender chunks of steak seasoned and cooked to perfection in the air fryer. They make for a quick, delicious snack or a great addition to a meal.

Tools needed:

- Ninja Air Fryer Pro
- Mixing bowls
- Air fryer basket
- Cooking spray

Ingredients:

- 1 pound sirloin steak, cut into bite-sized cubes
- 2 tablespoons olive oil
- 1 teaspoon garlic powder
- 1 teaspoon onion powder
- 1 teaspoon dried rosemary
- 1/2 teaspoon smoked paprika
- Salt and pepper to taste

Direction:

1. Preheat the air fryer to 400°F (200°C).
2. In a bowl, toss the steak cubes with olive oil, garlic powder, onion powder, rosemary, smoked paprika, salt, and pepper.
3. Place the steak cubes in the air fryer basket in a single layer.
4. Air fry for 8-10 minutes, shaking the basket halfway through, until the steak bites are crispy on the outside and cooked to your desired doneness.
5. Serve hot with your favorite dipping sauce or as a topping for salads and sandwiches.

Servings: 4 | **Prep time:** 10 minutes | **Cooking time:** 8-10 minutes

Nutritional info (per serving, 4 oz):
Calories: 250
Protein: 28g
Fat: 14g
Carbohydrates: 1g
Sugar: 0g

Quick tips:

- For even cooking, avoid overcrowding the air fryer basket.
- Let the steak bites rest for a few minutes before serving to allow juices to redistribute.

BBQ Beef Meatballs are a delicious, savory snack or meal that gets a crispy exterior from the air fryer while remaining juicy inside. Coated in a tangy barbecue sauce, these meatballs are perfect for game day or a quick dinner.

Tools needed:

Ninja Air Fryer Pro
Mixing bowls
Air fryer basket
Cooking spray

Ingredients:

For the Meatballs:

- 1 pound ground beef
- 1/2 cup breadcrumbs
- 1/4 cup finely chopped onion
- 1/4 cup grated Parmesan cheese
- 1 large egg
- 2 cloves garlic, minced
- 1 tablespoon chopped fresh parsley
- Salt and pepper to taste

For the BBQ Sauce:

- 1/2 cup barbecue sauce
- 2 tablespoons honey
- 1 tablespoon apple cider vinegar

Direction:

1. Preheat the air fryer to 400°F (200°C).
2. In a large bowl, combine ground beef, breadcrumbs, onion, Parmesan cheese, egg, garlic, parsley, salt, and pepper. Mix until well combined.
3. Form the mixture into meatballs, about 1-inch in diameter.
4. Spray the air fryer basket with cooking spray and place the meatballs in the basket in a single layer.
5. Air fry for 10-12 minutes, shaking the basket halfway through, until the meatballs are cooked through and browned.
6. While meatballs are cooking, mix barbecue sauce, honey, and apple cider vinegar in a small bowl.
7. Toss the cooked meatballs in the BBQ sauce before serving.

Servings: 4 | **Prep time:** 15 minutes | **Cooking time:** 10-12 minutes

Nutritional info (per serving, 4 meatballs):
Calories: 280
Protein: 20g
Fat: 15g
Carbohydrates: 15g
Sugar: 10g

Quick tips:

- For a different flavor, try using your favorite barbecue sauce or add extra spices to the meatball mixture.
- Make sure the meatballs are evenly spaced in the air fryer basket for consistent cooking.

Air Fryer Cheeseburger Sliders are mini burgers with melted cheese and all the classic toppings, cooked quickly and easily in the air fryer. Perfect for parties or a fun meal with family.

Tools needed:

- Ninja Air Fryer Pro
- Mixing bowls
- Air fryer basket
- Cooking spray

Ingredients:

For the Sliders:

- 1 pound ground beef
- 1/2 teaspoon garlic powder
- 1/2 teaspoon onion powder
- Salt and pepper to taste
- 6 slider buns
- 6 slices cheddar cheese
- Pickles, ketchup, and mustard for serving

Direction:

1. Preheat the air fryer to 375°F (190°C).
2. In a bowl, season the ground beef with garlic powder, onion powder, salt, and pepper. Mix until combined.
3. Divide the mixture into 6 equal portions and shape into slider patties.
4. Spray the air fryer basket with cooking spray and place the patties in the basket, ensuring they don't touch.
5. Air fry for 8-10 minutes, flipping halfway through, until the patties are cooked to your desired doneness.
6. Place a slice of cheddar cheese on each patty during the last minute of cooking.
7. Toast the slider buns in the air fryer for 1-2 minutes if desired.
8. Assemble sliders with pickles, ketchup, and mustard.

Servings: 6 | **Prep time:** 10 minutes | **Cooking time:** 8-10 minutes

Nutritional info (per slider): Calories: 250, Protein: 18g, Fat: 15g, Carbohydrates: 14g, Sugar: 3g

Quick tips:

- For extra flavor, add a slice of tomato or a few leaves of lettuce.
- Make sure not to overcrowd the air fryer basket to ensure even cooking.

Pepper-Crusted Roast Beef is a flavorful and elegant dish featuring a crispy pepper crust and tender, juicy beef. The air fryer makes it easy to cook a perfectly roasted beef with minimal effort.

Tools needed:

- Ninja Air Fryer Pro
- Mixing bowls
- Air fryer basket
- Meat thermometer

Ingredients:

- 2-pound beef roast (such as ribeye or sirloin)
- 2 tablespoons olive oil
- 2 tablespoons coarsely ground black pepper
- 1 tablespoon garlic powder
- 1 tablespoon onion powder
- 1 teaspoon salt
- 1 teaspoon dried thyme

Direction:

1. Preheat the air fryer to 400°F (200°C).
2. Rub the beef roast with olive oil, then season with black pepper, garlic powder, onion powder, salt, and thyme.
3. Place the beef roast in the air fryer basket.
4. Air fry for 20-25 minutes, or until the internal temperature reaches 135°F (57°C) for medium-rare, or longer for desired doneness.
5. Remove the roast from the air fryer and let it rest for 10 minutes before slicing.

Servings: 4 | **Prep time:** 10 minutes | **Cooking time:** 20-25 minutes

Nutritional info (per serving, 4 oz):
Calories: 280
Protein: 30g
Fat: 17g
Carbohydrates: 1g
Sugar: 0g

Quick tips:

- Let the roast rest before slicing to keep it juicy.
- Adjust cooking time based on the size of the roast and desired level of doneness.

Mongolian Beef Strips are tender beef pieces coated in a savory and slightly sweet sauce, all cooked to perfection in the air fryer. This dish offers the rich flavors of Mongolian cuisine with a crispy twist.

Tools needed:

Ninja Air Fryer Pro
Mixing bowls
Air fryer basket
Cooking spray

Ingredients:

For the Beef:

- 1 pound flank steak, thinly sliced into strips
- 2 tablespoons soy sauce
- 1 tablespoon cornstarch
- 1 tablespoon vegetable oil

For the Sauce:

- 1/4 cup soy sauce
- 1/4 cup brown sugar
- 1/4 cup water
- 2 cloves garlic, minced
- 1 teaspoon ginger, minced
- 1 tablespoon hoisin sauce
- 1 tablespoon rice vinegar
- 1 tablespoon sesame oil
- 2 green onions, sliced (for garnish)

Direction:

1. Preheat the air fryer to 400°F (200°C).

2. In a bowl, toss the beef strips with soy sauce, cornstarch, and vegetable oil until evenly coated.
3. Arrange the beef strips in a single layer in the air fryer basket.
4. Air fry for 8-10 minutes, shaking the basket halfway through, until the beef is crispy and cooked through.
5. While the beef is cooking, prepare the sauce by combining soy sauce, brown sugar, water, garlic, ginger, hoisin sauce, rice vinegar, and sesame oil in a small saucepan. Bring to a simmer over medium heat until slightly thickened.
6. Toss the cooked beef strips in the sauce and garnish with sliced green onions before serving.

Servings: 4 | **Prep time:** 15 minutes | **Cooking time:** 8-10 minutes

Nutritional info (per serving, 4 oz beef with sauce):
Calories: 290
Protein: 23g
Fat: 14g
Carbohydrates: 23g
Sugar: 14g

Quick tips:

- For extra crispiness, pat the beef strips dry before tossing with cornstarch.
- Adjust the sauce thickness by simmering longer or adding a bit more water.

Korean BBQ Beef Ribs

Korean BBQ Beef Ribs are flavorful and tender, with a caramelized glaze that comes from a combination of sweet and savory Korean spices. The air fryer ensures a crispy exterior while keeping the ribs juicy.

Tools needed:

Ninja Air Fryer Pro
Mixing bowls
Air fryer basket
Cooking spray

Ingredients:

For the Ribs:

- 2 pounds beef short ribs, cut into individual pieces
- 1/4 cup soy sauce
- 2 tablespoons brown sugar
- 2 tablespoons rice vinegar
- 2 tablespoons honey
- 2 cloves garlic, minced
- 1 teaspoon ginger, minced
- 1 tablespoon sesame oil
- 1 tablespoon Gochujang (Korean red chili paste)
- 1 tablespoon sesame seeds (for garnish)
- 2 green onions, sliced (for garnish)

Direction:

1. Preheat the air fryer to 380°F (193°C).
2. In a bowl, mix soy sauce, brown sugar, rice vinegar, honey, garlic, ginger, sesame oil, and Gochujang.
3. Marinate the beef ribs in the mixture for at least 1 hour or overnight in the refrigerator.
4. Spray the air fryer basket with cooking spray and place the marinated ribs in a single layer.
5. Air fry for 15-18 minutes, flipping halfway through, until the ribs are crispy and cooked through.
6. Garnish with sesame seeds and sliced green onions before serving.

Servings: 4 | **Prep time:** 15 minutes | **Marinating time:** 1 hour | **Cooking time:** 15-18 minutes

Nutritional info: Calories: 350, Protein: 25g, Fat: 24g, Carbohydrates: 20g, Sugar: 14g
Quick tips:

For best results, marinate the ribs overnight to enhance the flavors.

Air Fried Beef Chimichangas are crispy, golden-brown burritos filled with seasoned beef and melted cheese. The air fryer makes these chimichangas delightfully crispy without the need for deep frying.

Tools needed:

Ninja Air Fryer Pro
Mixing bowls
Air fryer basket
Cooking spray

Ingredients:

For the Filling:

- 1 pound ground beef
- 1 small onion, chopped
- 1 clove garlic, minced
- 1 tablespoon taco seasoning
- 1/2 cup shredded cheddar cheese
- 1/4 cup chopped cilantro
- 1/4 cup sour cream

For Assembly:

- 6 large flour tortillas
- Cooking spray

Direction:

1. Preheat the air fryer to 400°F (200°C).
2. In a skillet, cook ground beef with onion and garlic until browned. Drain excess fat.
3. Stir in taco seasoning and cook for another 2 minutes. Remove from heat and mix in cheddar cheese, cilantro, and sour cream.
4. Spoon the beef mixture into the center of each tortilla and roll up, folding in the sides to enclose the filling.
5. Spray the air fryer basket with cooking spray and place the chimichangas seam-side down in the basket.
6. Air fry for 8-10 minutes, turning halfway through, until the chimichangas are crispy and golden brown.

Servings: 6 | **Prep time:** 15 minutes | **Cooking time:** 8-10 minutes

Nutritional info: Calories: 350, Protein: 20g, Fat: 18g, Carbohydrates: 30g, Sugar: 2g
Quick tips:

- To prevent the chimichangas from unrolling, make sure the seam is secured well.

AIRFRYER PORK RECIPES

Air Fryer Pork Chops

Air Fryer Pork Chops are juicy and tender with a crispy exterior, achieved quickly and easily in the air fryer. This recipe is perfect for a weeknight dinner or a special occasion.

Tools needed:

- Ninja Air Fryer Pro
- Mixing bowls
- Air fryer basket
- Cooking spray

Ingredients:

- 4 bone-in or boneless pork chops, about 1-inch thick
- 2 tablespoons olive oil
- 1 teaspoon garlic powder
- 1 teaspoon onion powder
- 1 teaspoon paprika
- 1/2 teaspoon dried thyme
- Salt and pepper to taste

Direction:

1. Preheat the air fryer to 400°F (200°C).
2. Rub the pork chops with olive oil, then season with garlic powder, onion powder, paprika, thyme, salt, and pepper.
3. Spray the air fryer basket with cooking spray and place the pork chops in the basket, making sure they do not overlap.
4. Air fry for 12-15 minutes, flipping halfway through, until the pork chops reach an internal temperature of 145°F (63°C) and are crispy on the outside.
5. Let the pork chops rest for a few minutes before serving.

Servings: 4 | **Prep time:** 10 minutes | **Cooking time:** 12-15 minutes

Nutritional info (per pork chop, without additional oil):
Calories: 280
Protein: 30g
Fat: 15g
Carbohydrates: 1g
Sugar: 0g

Quick tips:

- Use a meat thermometer to ensure the pork chops are cooked to the proper temperature.
- For extra crispiness, pat the pork chops dry before seasoning.

BBQ Pulled Pork Sandwiches feature tender, flavorful pulled pork with a smoky barbecue sauce, served on soft buns. The air fryer makes the pork deliciously juicy while keeping it easy to prepare.

Tools needed:

Ninja Air Fryer Pro
Mixing bowls
Air fryer basket
Slow cooker or Instant Pot (for initial cooking)
Cooking spray

Ingredients:

For the Pulled Pork:

- 2 pounds pork shoulder (or pork butt)
- 1/4 cup barbecue rub
- 1/2 cup apple cider vinegar
- 1 cup barbecue sauce

For Assembly:

- 6 hamburger buns
- Coleslaw (optional, for topping)
- Extra barbecue sauce (optional)

Direction:

1. Rub the pork shoulder with barbecue rub and place it in a slow cooker or Instant Pot with apple cider vinegar. Cook on low for 8 hours (slow cooker) or 60 minutes (Instant Pot) until the pork is tender and easy to shred.
2. Remove the pork from the cooker and shred it with two forks. Mix in the barbecue sauce.
3. Preheat the air fryer to 360°F (182°C).
4. Place the shredded pork in the air fryer basket and air fry for 5-7 minutes to get a slightly crispy edge, shaking the basket halfway through.
5. Serve the pulled pork on hamburger buns with optional coleslaw and extra barbecue sauce.

Servings: 6 | **Prep time:** 15 minutes (plus slow cooking time) | **Cooking time:** 5-7 minutes

Nutritional info (per sandwich, with bun and sauce): Calories: 400, Protein: 25g, Fat: 18g, Carbohydrates: 35g, Sugar: 14g

Quick tips:

- Use a lean cut of pork shoulder for less fat.
- For added flavor, try marinating the pork overnight before cooking.

Crispy Air Fryer Bacon is a simple and efficient way to cook bacon to perfection. The air fryer ensures evenly cooked, crispy bacon with less mess and less fat.

Tools needed:

- Ninja Air Fryer Pro
- Air fryer basket
- Paper towels

Ingredients:

- 8 strips of bacon

Direction:

1. Preheat the air fryer to 400°F (200°C).
2. Arrange the bacon strips in a single layer in the air fryer basket. You may need to cook in batches depending on the size of your air fryer.
3. Air fry for 8-10 minutes, flipping halfway through, until the bacon is crispy and golden brown.
4. Remove the bacon and drain on paper towels to remove excess grease.

Servings: 4 | **Prep time:** 5 minutes | **Cooking time:** 8-10 minutes

Nutritional info (per strip):
Calories: 42
Protein: 3g
Fat: 3g
Carbohydrates: 0g
Sugar: 0g

Quick tips:

- For crispier bacon, add an extra minute or two to the cooking time.
- If cooking multiple batches, allow the air fryer to cool slightly between batches to prevent smoke.

Air Fryer Pork Belly Bites

Air Fryer Pork Belly Bites are succulent and crispy pieces of pork belly that are perfect for snacking or as an appetizer. The air fryer ensures a crispy exterior while keeping the pork belly tender and juicy.

Tools needed:

- Ninja Air Fryer Pro
- Mixing bowls
- Air fryer basket
- Cooking spray

Ingredients:

- 1 pound pork belly, cut into bite-sized pieces
- 2 tablespoons soy sauce
- 1 tablespoon honey
- 1 tablespoon rice vinegar
- 1 teaspoon five-spice powder
- 1 teaspoon garlic powder
- Salt and pepper to taste

Direction:

1. Preheat the air fryer to 400°F (200°C).
2. In a bowl, combine soy sauce, honey, rice vinegar, five-spice powder, garlic powder, salt, and pepper.
3. Toss the pork belly pieces in the marinade until well coated.
4. Spray the air fryer basket with cooking spray and place the pork belly pieces in a single layer.
5. Air fry for 15-20 minutes, shaking the basket halfway through, until the pork belly is crispy and cooked through.
6. Remove from the air fryer and let rest for a few minutes before serving.

Servings: 4 | **Prep time:** 10 minutes | **Cooking time:** 15-20 minutes

Nutritional info (per serving, 4 oz):
Calories: 400
Protein: 18g
Fat: 30g
Carbohydrates: 12g
Sugar: 8g

Quick tips:

- Cut the pork belly into uniform pieces for even cooking.
- For extra crispiness, pat the pork belly dry before marinating.

Garlic Parmesan Pork Tenderloin

Garlic Parmesan Pork Tenderloin is a flavorful and juicy pork dish with a crispy garlic Parmesan coating. Cooked in the air fryer, it's easy to prepare and perfect for a quick, delicious dinner.

Tools needed:

- Ninja Air Fryer Pro
- Mixing bowls
- Air fryer basket
- Cooking spray

Ingredients:

- 1 pound pork tenderloin
- 1 tablespoon olive oil
- 1/4 cup grated Parmesan cheese
- 2 cloves garlic, minced
- 1 teaspoon dried Italian seasoning
- 1/2 teaspoon paprika
- Salt and pepper to taste

Direction:

1. Preheat the air fryer to 400°F (200°C).
2. Rub the pork tenderloin with olive oil.
3. In a bowl, mix Parmesan cheese, minced garlic, Italian seasoning, paprika, salt, and pepper.
4. Coat the pork tenderloin with the Parmesan mixture, pressing gently to adhere.
5. Spray the air fryer basket with cooking spray and place the pork tenderloin in the basket.
6. Air fry for 20-25 minutes, or until the internal temperature reaches 145°F (63°C) and the coating is golden and crispy.
7. Let the pork tenderloin rest for 5 minutes before slicing.

Servings: 4 | **Prep time:** 10 minutes | **Cooking time:** 20-25 minutes

Nutritional info (per serving, 4 oz):
Calories: 250
Protein: 30g
Fat: 12g
Carbohydrates: 2g
Sugar: 0g

Quick tips:

- For an even coating, press the Parmesan mixture onto the pork tenderloin firmly.
- Let the pork tenderloin rest to retain its juices and ensure a tender result.

Sweet and Sour Pork

Sweet and Sour Pork is a classic dish with crispy pork pieces coated in a tangy and sweet sauce. The air fryer provides a healthier alternative to deep frying while still achieving a deliciously crispy texture.

Tools needed:

Ninja Air Fryer Pro
Mixing bowls
Air fryer basket
Saucepan (for sauce)

Ingredients:

For the Pork:

- 1 pound pork loin, cut into bite-sized pieces
- 1/2 cup cornstarch
- 1/2 cup flour
- 1 egg, beaten
- Cooking spray

For the Sauce:

- 1/2 cup ketchup
- 1/4 cup rice vinegar
- 1/4 cup brown sugar
- 1 tablespoon soy sauce
- 1 teaspoon minced garlic
- 1 teaspoon minced ginger

Direction:

1. Preheat the air fryer to 400°F (200°C).
2. In one bowl, mix cornstarch and flour. In another bowl, place the beaten egg.
3. Dip each pork piece first in the egg, then in the cornstarch mixture, coating evenly.
4. Spray the air fryer basket with cooking spray and place the coated pork pieces in a single layer.
5. Air fry for 12-15 minutes, shaking the basket halfway through, until the pork is crispy and cooked through.
6. While the pork is cooking, prepare the sauce by combining ketchup, rice vinegar, brown sugar, soy sauce, garlic, and ginger in a saucepan. Simmer over medium heat until the sauce thickens.
7. Toss the cooked pork in the sweet and sour sauce before serving.

Servings: 4 | **Prep time:** 15 minutes | **Cooking time:** 12-15 minutes

Nutritional info (per serving, 4 oz with sauce):
Calories: 350
Protein: 25g
Fat: 15g
Carbohydrates: 30g
Sugar: 20g

Quick tips:

- Ensure the pork pieces are coated evenly for a consistent crispiness.
- Adjust the sweetness or tanginess of the sauce to your preference by modifying the sugar or vinegar amounts.

Air Fryer Sausage Links are a quick and easy way to cook sausages with a crisp exterior and juicy interior. The air fryer ensures that the sausages are cooked evenly without needing to use excess oil.

Tools needed:

- Ninja Air Fryer Pro
- Air fryer basket
- Cooking spray

Ingredients:

- 6 sausage links (pork, chicken, or turkey)

Direction:

1. Preheat the air fryer to 400°F (200°C).
2. Spray the air fryer basket with cooking spray.
3. Arrange the sausage links in a single layer in the air fryer basket, making sure they are not overcrowded.
4. Air fry for 10-12 minutes, turning halfway through, until the sausages are golden brown and cooked through. They should reach an internal temperature of 160°F (71°C).
5. Let the sausages rest for a few minutes before serving.

Servings: 6 | **Prep time:** 5 minutes | **Cooking time:** 10-12 minutes

Nutritional info (per sausage link, average):
Calories: 180
Protein: 12g
Fat: 15g
Carbohydrates: 2g
Sugar: 1g

Quick tips:

- If cooking different types of sausages, check the internal temperature to ensure they are fully cooked.
- For extra flavor, you can marinate the sausages before air frying.

Honey Mustard Glazed Ham is a delicious and flavorful dish with a sweet and tangy glaze. The air fryer helps to caramelize the glaze and give the ham a beautiful golden finish.

Tools needed:

- Ninja Air Fryer Pro
- Mixing bowls
- Air fryer basket
- Cooking brush

Ingredients:

- 1 pound ham steak
- 1/4 cup honey
- 2 tablespoons Dijon mustard
- 1 tablespoon brown sugar
- 1 teaspoon apple cider vinegar
- 1/2 teaspoon garlic powder

Direction:

1. Preheat the air fryer to 380°F (193°C).
2. In a bowl, mix honey, Dijon mustard, brown sugar, apple cider vinegar, and garlic powder to create the glaze.
3. Brush the ham steak with the glaze, coating it evenly.
4. Spray the air fryer basket with cooking spray and place the glazed ham steak in the basket.
5. Air fry for 10-12 minutes, brushing with additional glaze halfway through, until the ham is heated through and caramelized.
6. Let the ham steak rest for a few minutes before slicing.

Servings: 4 | **Prep time:** 10 minutes | **Cooking time:** 10-12 minutes

Nutritional info (per serving, 4 oz):
Calories: 250
Protein: 20g
Fat: 10g
Carbohydrates: 20g
Sugar: 18g

Quick tips:

- For a more intense glaze, brush on extra honey and mustard before the final few minutes of cooking.
- Ensure the ham steak is fully coated with the glaze for a more flavorful result.

Air Fried Pork Schnitzel is a classic dish with a crispy breadcrumb coating and tender pork. The air fryer provides a healthier alternative to deep frying while maintaining that satisfying crunch.

Tools needed:

- Ninja Air Fryer Pro
- Mixing bowls
- Air fryer basket
- Cooking spray
- Meat mallet or rolling pin

Ingredients:

- 4 pork cutlets (about 1/2 inch thick)
- 1/2 cup all-purpose flour
- 2 large eggs, beaten
- 1 cup breadcrumbs
- 1/2 cup grated Parmesan cheese
- 1 teaspoon paprika
- 1 teaspoon garlic powder
- Salt and pepper to taste
- Cooking spray

Direction:

1. Preheat the air fryer to 400°F (200°C).
2. Place each pork cutlet between two sheets of plastic wrap and pound with a meat mallet or rolling pin to an even thickness.
3. In a bowl, mix flour with salt and pepper. In another bowl, place beaten eggs. In a third bowl, mix breadcrumbs, Parmesan cheese, paprika, and garlic powder.
4. Dredge each pork cutlet first in the flour, then dip in the beaten eggs, and coat with the breadcrumb mixture.
5. Spray the air fryer basket with cooking spray and place the breaded pork cutlets in the basket in a single layer.
6. Air fry for 10-12 minutes, flipping halfway through, until the schnitzel is golden brown and crispy.
7. Serve immediately with lemon wedges and your favorite side dishes.

Servings: 4 | **Prep time:** 15 minutes | **Cooking time:** 10-12 minutes

Nutritional info (per schnitzel, without sides): Calories: 350, Protein: 30g, Fat: 20g, Carbohydrates: 20g, Sugar: 2g

Quick tips:

- For an extra crispy coating, double-dip the schnitzels in egg and breadcrumbs.
- Ensure the pork cutlets are of even thickness for uniform cooking.

Maple Glazed Bacon Wrapped Asparagus combines the savory taste of bacon with the freshness of asparagus, all caramelized with a sweet maple glaze. This appetizer or side dish is quick and easy to make in the air fryer.

Tools needed:

- Ninja Air Fryer Pro
- Mixing bowls
- Air fryer basket
- Toothpicks or skewers
- Cooking spray

Ingredients:

- 12 asparagus spears, trimmed
- 6 strips of bacon, cut in half
- 2 tablespoons maple syrup
- 1 tablespoon Dijon mustard
- 1 tablespoon olive oil
- Salt and pepper to taste

Direction:

1. Preheat the air fryer to 375°F (190°C).
2. In a small bowl, mix maple syrup, Dijon mustard, and olive oil.
3. Wrap each asparagus spear with a half strip of bacon and secure with a toothpick or skewer.
4. Brush the bacon-wrapped asparagus with the maple glaze mixture and season with salt and pepper.
5. Spray the air fryer basket with cooking spray and arrange the wrapped asparagus in a single layer.
6. Air fry for 10-12 minutes, flipping halfway through, until the bacon is crispy and the asparagus is tender.
7. Remove the toothpicks or skewers before serving.

Servings: 4 | **Prep time:** 10 minutes | **Cooking time:** 10-12 minutes

Nutritional info (per serving, 3 pieces): Calories: 150, Protein: 6g, Fat: 12g, Carbohydrates: 6g, Sugar: 4g

Quick tips:

- For a crispier bacon, ensure the bacon is fully wrapped and secured around the asparagus.
- Adjust the maple syrup quantity to your desired level of sweetness.

AIRFRYER MEDITERRANEAN RECIPES

Air Fryer Falafel

Air Fryer Falafel is a healthier take on the classic Middle Eastern chickpea fritters. Crispy on the outside and tender on the inside, these falafels are perfect for a snack or as part of a meal.

Tools needed:

Ninja Air Fryer Pro
Food processor
Mixing bowls
Air fryer basket
Cooking spray

Ingredients:

- 1 can (15 oz) chickpeas, drained and rinsed
- 1/2 cup fresh parsley, chopped
- 1/2 cup fresh cilantro, chopped
- 1 small onion, chopped
- 3 cloves garlic, minced
- 1 teaspoon ground cumin
- 1 teaspoon ground coriander
- 1/2 teaspoon baking powder
- Salt and pepper to taste
- 2 tablespoons flour
- Cooking spray

Direction:

1. Preheat the air fryer to 400°F (200°C).
2. In a food processor, combine chickpeas, parsley, cilantro, onion, garlic, cumin, coriander, baking powder, salt, and pepper. Pulse until a coarse mixture forms.
3. Add flour and pulse again until the mixture holds together. If needed, add a bit more flour.
4. Shape the mixture into small balls or patties.
5. Spray the air fryer basket with cooking spray and arrange the falafel balls in a single layer.
6. Air fry for 10-12 minutes, shaking the basket halfway through, until golden brown and crispy.
7. Serve with pita bread, hummus, or a fresh salad.

Servings: 4 | **Prep time:** 15 minutes | **Cooking time:** 10-12 minutes

Nutritional info (per serving, 4 pieces):
Calories: 200
Protein: 8g
Fat: 7g
Carbohydrates: 25g
Sugar: 4g

Quick tips:

- For a smoother mixture, process the ingredients until very finely chopped.
- If the mixture is too dry, add a splash of water to help it bind.

Greek Lemon Chicken Skewers are marinated in a zesty lemon and herb mixture, then cooked to perfection in the air fryer. They're ideal for a flavorful and easy-to-make dinner or appetizer.

Tools needed:

- Ninja Air Fryer Pro
- Mixing bowls
- Skewers
- Air fryer basket
- Cooking spray

Ingredients:

- 1 pound chicken breast, cut into bite-sized pieces
- 1/4 cup olive oil
- Juice of 1 lemon
- 2 cloves garlic, minced
- 1 tablespoon dried oregano
- 1 teaspoon paprika
- Salt and pepper to taste
- Wooden or metal skewers

Direction:

1. Preheat the air fryer to 400°F (200°C).
2. In a bowl, mix olive oil, lemon juice, garlic, oregano, paprika, salt, and pepper.
3. Add the chicken pieces to the marinade and toss to coat. Marinate for at least 30 minutes.
4. Thread the marinated chicken onto skewers.
5. Spray the air fryer basket with cooking spray and place the skewers in the basket.
6. Air fry for 10-12 minutes, turning halfway through, until the chicken is cooked through and slightly charred.
7. Serve with tzatziki sauce and a side of Greek salad.

Servings: 4 | **Prep time:** 15 minutes (plus marinating time) | **Cooking time:** 10-12 minutes

Nutritional info (per serving, 2 skewers): Calories: 220, Protein: 30g, Fat: 12g, Carbohydrates: 1g, Sugar: 0g

Quick tips:

- For juicier chicken, don't overcook the skewers. Check for doneness with a meat thermometer.
- If using wooden skewers, soak them in water for 30 minutes before using to prevent burning.

Air Fried Spanakopita

Air Fried Spanakopita is a delicious Greek pastry featuring a crispy, golden-brown crust filled with a savory mixture of spinach and feta cheese. The air fryer makes it easy to achieve that perfect crunch without needing to use excess oil.

Tools needed:

- Ninja Air Fryer Pro
- Mixing bowls
- Air fryer basket
- Cooking spray
- Pastry brush

Ingredients:

- 8 sheets phyllo dough, thawed
- 1/4 cup melted butter or olive oil
- 2 cups fresh spinach, chopped
- 1 cup feta cheese, crumbled
- 1/2 cup ricotta cheese
- 1 small onion, finely chopped
- 2 cloves garlic, minced
- 1 egg, beaten
- Salt and pepper to taste

Direction:

1. Preheat the air fryer to 350°F (175°C).
2. In a bowl, mix the spinach, feta cheese, ricotta cheese, onion, garlic, beaten egg, salt, and pepper.
3. Brush a phyllo sheet with melted butter or olive oil and place another sheet on top, repeating this process to layer 4 sheets.
4. Spoon the spinach mixture onto the bottom of the layered phyllo dough.
5. Fold the edges of the phyllo dough over the filling and roll it up to form a log or spiral shape.
6. Brush the top with more melted butter or olive oil.
7. Place the spanakopita in the air fryer basket and cook for 15-20 minutes, or until golden brown and crispy.
8. Let cool slightly before slicing and serving.

Servings: 4 | **Prep time:** 15 minutes | **Cooking time:** 15-20 minutes

Nutritional info (per serving, 1/4 of the recipe): Calories: 300, Protein: 10g, Fat: 20g, Carbohydrates: 20g, Sugar: 3g
Quick tips:

- Make sure to keep the phyllo dough covered with a damp towel while working to prevent it from drying out.

Mediterranean Stuffed Bell Peppers are a colorful and nutritious dish filled with a blend of rice, vegetables, and spices. Cooked in the air fryer, they come out tender and perfectly cooked, with a delightful, slightly crispy top.

Tools needed:

- Ninja Air Fryer Pro
- Mixing bowls
- Air fryer basket
- Cooking spray

Ingredients:

- 4 large bell peppers (any color), tops cut off and seeds removed
- 1 cup cooked rice (white or brown)
- 1/2 cup cooked chickpeas
- 1/2 cup diced tomatoes
- 1/4 cup Kalamata olives, chopped
- 1/4 cup crumbled feta cheese
- 1 teaspoon dried oregano
- 1 teaspoon dried basil
- 1 tablespoon olive oil
- Salt and pepper to taste

Direction:

1. Preheat the air fryer to 360°F (182°C).
2. In a bowl, mix cooked rice, chickpeas, diced tomatoes, olives, feta cheese, oregano, basil, olive oil, salt, and pepper.
3. Stuff each bell pepper with the rice mixture, pressing down gently to pack the filling.
4. Spray the air fryer basket with cooking spray and place the stuffed peppers upright in the basket.
5. Air fry for 15-18 minutes, or until the peppers are tender and the tops are slightly crispy.
6. Serve hot with a side of tzatziki sauce or a fresh salad.

Servings: 4 | **Prep time:** 10 minutes | **Cooking time:** 15-18 minutes

Nutritional info (per stuffed pepper): Calories: 220, Protein: 8g, Fat: 10g, Carbohydrates: 25g, Sugar: 7g

Quick tips:

- For added flavor, you can sprinkle some extra feta cheese or fresh herbs on top before air frying.
- If the peppers are too large, cut off the bottoms slightly to ensure they sit upright in the basket.

Air Fryer Lamb Kofta

Air Fryer Lamb Kofta is a flavorful Middle Eastern dish made from ground lamb mixed with spices and herbs, then shaped into kebabs. The air fryer makes them perfectly juicy and crispy on the outside, with minimal oil.

Tools needed:

- Ninja Air Fryer Pro
- Mixing bowls
- Air fryer basket
- Skewers (if desired)
- Cooking spray

Ingredients:

- 1 pound ground lamb
- 1/2 cup onion, finely chopped
- 2 cloves garlic, minced
- 1/4 cup fresh parsley, chopped
- 1/4 cup fresh cilantro, chopped
- 1 teaspoon ground cumin
- 1 teaspoon ground coriander
- 1/2 teaspoon paprika
- 1/2 teaspoon ground cinnamon
- Salt and pepper to taste
- Cooking spray

Direction:

1. Preheat the air fryer to 400°F (200°C).
2. In a bowl, combine ground lamb, onion, garlic, parsley, cilantro, cumin, coriander, paprika, cinnamon, salt, and pepper. Mix well.
3. Shape the mixture into small patties or form onto skewers if using.
4. Spray the air fryer basket with cooking spray and place the kofta in the basket in a single layer.
5. Air fry for 10-12 minutes, turning halfway through, until the kofta is cooked through and crispy on the outside.
6. Serve with pita bread, hummus, or a fresh salad.

Servings: 4 | **Prep time:** 15 minutes | **Cooking time:** 10-12 minutes

Nutritional info (per serving, 2 kofta patties): Calories: 250, Protein: 20g, Fat: 18g, Carbohydrates: 5g, Sugar: 1g

Quick tips:

- For more uniform cooking, ensure the kofta patties are of similar size and thickness.
- Let the kofta rest for a few minutes before serving to help retain its juices.

Garlic Herb Air Fried Shrimp are succulent shrimp seasoned with garlic and fresh herbs, then cooked to perfection in the air fryer. They are quick to prepare and make a delightful appetizer or main dish.

Tools needed:

- Ninja Air Fryer Pro
- Mixing bowls
- Air fryer basket
- Cooking spray

Ingredients:

- 1 pound large shrimp, peeled and deveined
- 2 tablespoons olive oil
- 3 cloves garlic, minced
- 1 tablespoon fresh parsley, chopped
- 1 teaspoon dried oregano
- 1/2 teaspoon paprika
- Salt and pepper to taste
- Lemon wedges, for serving

Direction:

1. Preheat the air fryer to 400°F (200°C).
2. In a bowl, toss the shrimp with olive oil, garlic, parsley, oregano, paprika, salt, and pepper until well coated.
3. Spray the air fryer basket with cooking spray and arrange the shrimp in a single layer.
4. Air fry for 6-8 minutes, shaking the basket halfway through, until the shrimp are cooked through and have a golden-brown exterior.
5. Serve with lemon wedges.

Servings: 4 | **Prep time:** 10 minutes | **Cooking time:** 6-8 minutes

Nutritional info (per serving, 6 shrimp):
Calories: 150
Protein: 20g
Fat: 6g
Carbohydrates: 2g
Sugar: 1g

Quick tips:

- For an extra burst of flavor, squeeze additional lemon juice over the shrimp before serving.
- Ensure the shrimp are not overcrowded in the basket to allow for even cooking.

Crispy Eggplant Parmesan

Crispy Eggplant Parmesan features tender slices of eggplant coated in a seasoned breadcrumb mixture and air-fried to a crispy perfection. This classic Italian dish is lighter and healthier when made in the air fryer.

Tools needed:

- Ninja Air Fryer Pro
- Mixing bowls
- Air fryer basket
- Cooking spray
- Shallow dishes for breading

Ingredients:

- 1 large eggplant, sliced into 1/2-inch rounds
- 1 cup all-purpose flour
- 2 large eggs, beaten
- 1 cup breadcrumbs
- 1/2 cup grated Parmesan cheese
- 1 cup marinara sauce
- 1 cup shredded mozzarella cheese
- 1 teaspoon dried basil
- 1 teaspoon dried oregano
- Salt and pepper to taste

Direction:

1. Preheat the air fryer to 380°F (193°C).
2. Set up a breading station with flour, beaten eggs, and a mixture of breadcrumbs, Parmesan cheese, dried basil, and oregano.
3. Dip each eggplant slice into the flour, then the beaten eggs, and finally coat with the breadcrumb mixture.
4. Spray the air fryer basket with cooking spray and arrange the breaded eggplant slices in a single layer.
5. Air fry for 10-12 minutes, flipping halfway through, until golden and crispy.
6. Spoon a small amount of marinara sauce on each slice, top with shredded mozzarella cheese, and air fry for an additional 2-3 minutes until the cheese is melted and bubbly.
7. Serve hot with additional marinara sauce.

Servings: 4 | **Prep time:** 20 minutes | **Cooking time:** 12-15 minutes

Nutritional info : Calories: 250, Protein: 12g, Fat: 12g, Carbohydrates: 25g, Sugar: 7g

Quick tips:

- For even crispiness, avoid overlapping the eggplant slices in the air fryer.
- You can use whole wheat breadcrumbs for a healthier option.

Air Fryer Pita Chips are crispy and crunchy, perfect for dipping in creamy hummus. This easy recipe transforms store-bought pita bread into delicious chips with minimal effort and oil.

Tools needed:

- Ninja Air Fryer Pro
- Cutting board
- Knife
- Air fryer basket
- Cooking spray

Ingredients:

- 4 pita bread rounds
- 2 tablespoons olive oil
- 1 teaspoon garlic powder
- 1 teaspoon dried oregano
- 1/2 teaspoon paprika
- Salt to taste
- Hummus, for serving

Direction:

1. Preheat the air fryer to 350°F (175°C).
2. Cut the pita bread rounds into triangle wedges.
3. In a bowl, toss the pita wedges with olive oil, garlic powder, oregano, paprika, and salt.
4. Spray the air fryer basket with cooking spray and arrange the pita wedges in a single layer.
5. Air fry for 5-7 minutes, shaking the basket halfway through, until the chips are golden and crispy.
6. Serve warm with your favorite hummus.

Servings: 4 | **Prep time:** 5 minutes | **Cooking time:** 5-7 minutes

Nutritional info (per serving, 10 chips):
Calories: 180
Protein: 4g
Fat: 8g
Carbohydrates: 25g
Sugar: 2g

Quick tips:

- For extra flavor, sprinkle the chips with a bit of Parmesan cheese or herbs before air frying.
- Make sure the pita wedges are in a single layer for even cooking.

Mediterranean Chicken Meatballs are tender and flavorful, seasoned with classic Mediterranean herbs and spices. These meatballs are perfect for a healthy meal or as a flavorful addition to a variety of dishes.

Tools needed:

- Ninja Air Fryer Pro
- Mixing bowls
- Air fryer basket
- Cooking spray

Ingredients:

- 1 pound ground chicken
- 1/2 cup breadcrumbs
- 1/4 cup grated Parmesan cheese
- 1/4 cup fresh parsley, chopped
- 1/4 cup fresh mint, chopped
- 2 cloves garlic, minced
- 1 teaspoon dried oregano
- 1/2 teaspoon ground cumin
- 1/2 teaspoon paprika
- Salt and pepper to taste
- 1 egg, beaten

Direction:

1. Preheat the air fryer to 400°F (200°C).
2. In a bowl, combine ground chicken, breadcrumbs, Parmesan cheese, parsley, mint, garlic, oregano, cumin, paprika, salt, pepper, and beaten egg. Mix until well combined.
3. Shape the mixture into 1-inch meatballs and arrange them in a single layer in the air fryer basket.
4. Spray the meatballs lightly with cooking spray.
5. Air fry for 10-12 minutes, or until the meatballs are golden brown and cooked through, turning halfway through.
6. Serve with a side of tzatziki sauce or over a bed of rice or salad.

Servings: 4 | **Prep time:** 15 minutes | **Cooking time:** 10-12 minutes

Nutritional info (per serving, 4 meatballs): Calories: 220, Protein: 22g, Fat: 12g, Carbohydrates: 8g, Sugar: 2g

Quick tips:

- Ensure meatballs are of uniform size for even cooking.
- For extra flavor, you can add a pinch of red pepper flakes or lemon zest to the mixture.

Air Fried Greek Potatoes are seasoned with a blend of herbs and spices, resulting in crispy and flavorful potato wedges. This recipe is a perfect side dish to complement any Mediterranean meal.

Tools needed:

- Ninja Air Fryer Pro
- Cutting board
- Knife
- Mixing bowls
- Air fryer basket
- Cooking spray

Ingredients:

- 4 large potatoes, cut into wedges
- 2 tablespoons olive oil
- 1 tablespoon lemon juice
- 1 teaspoon dried oregano
- 1 teaspoon dried rosemary
- 1/2 teaspoon garlic powder
- Salt and pepper to taste
- Fresh parsley, for garnish

Direction:

1. Preheat the air fryer to 400°F (200°C).
2. In a bowl, toss the potato wedges with olive oil, lemon juice, oregano, rosemary, garlic powder, salt, and pepper until evenly coated.
3. Spray the air fryer basket with cooking spray and arrange the potato wedges in a single layer.
4. Air fry for 15-20 minutes, shaking the basket halfway through, until the potatoes are crispy and golden brown.
5. Garnish with fresh parsley before serving.

Servings: 4 | **Prep time:** 10 minutes | **Cooking time:** 15-20 minutes

Nutritional info (per serving, 1/4 of the recipe): Calories: 210, Protein: 3g, Fat: 10g, Carbohydrates: 30g, Sugar: 2g

Quick tips:

- For extra crispiness, soak the potato wedges in water for 30 minutes before cooking, then pat them dry thoroughly.
- Avoid overcrowding the air fryer basket to ensure even cooking.

AIRFRYER LAMB RECIPES

Air Fryer Lamb Chops

Air Fryer Lamb Chops are a succulent and flavorful dish that cooks quickly and evenly in the air fryer. The lamb is seasoned with a mix of herbs and spices, then air-fried to perfection.

Tools needed:

- Ninja Air Fryer Pro
- Mixing bowls
- Air fryer basket
- Cooking spray

Ingredients:

- 8 lamb chops
- 2 tablespoons olive oil
- 2 cloves garlic, minced
- 1 tablespoon fresh rosemary, chopped
- 1 tablespoon fresh thyme, chopped
- 1 teaspoon dried mint
- Salt and pepper to taste

Direction:

1. Preheat the air fryer to 400°F (200°C).
2. In a bowl, mix olive oil, garlic, rosemary, thyme, mint, salt, and pepper.
3. Rub the lamb chops with the seasoning mixture, ensuring they are well coated.
4. Spray the air fryer basket with cooking spray and place the lamb chops in a single layer.
5. Air fry for 8-10 minutes, turning halfway through, until the lamb chops are cooked to your desired level of doneness.
6. Let the lamb chops rest for a few minutes before serving.

Servings: 4 | **Prep time:** 10 minutes | **Cooking time:** 8-10 minutes

Nutritional info (per serving, 2 lamb chops):
Calories: 300
Protein: 25g
Fat: 20g
Carbohydrates: 1g
Sugar: 0g

Quick tips:

- For best results, allow the lamb chops to come to room temperature before cooking.
- Use a meat thermometer to ensure the lamb is cooked to your preferred level of doneness.

Spicy Lamb Kebabs are flavorful and juicy skewers of lamb seasoned with a blend of spices and herbs. Perfect for a BBQ or a flavorful dinner, these kebabs are cooked to perfection in the air fryer.

Tools needed:

- Ninja Air Fryer Pro
- Skewers (metal or soaked wooden)
- Mixing bowls
- Air fryer basket
- Cooking spray

Ingredients:

- 1 pound lamb shoulder or leg, cut into 1-inch cubes
- 2 tablespoons olive oil
- 2 teaspoons smoked paprika
- 1 teaspoon ground cumin
- 1 teaspoon ground coriander
- 1/2 teaspoon cayenne pepper (adjust to taste)
- 1 teaspoon garlic powder
- 1 teaspoon onion powder
- 1 teaspoon dried oregano
- Salt and pepper to taste
- Lemon wedges, for serving

Direction:

1. Preheat the air fryer to 400°F (200°C).
2. In a bowl, mix olive oil, smoked paprika, cumin, coriander, cayenne pepper, garlic powder, onion powder, oregano, salt, and pepper.
3. Toss the lamb cubes in the spice mixture until well coated.
4. Thread the lamb onto skewers.
5. Spray the air fryer basket with cooking spray and place the skewers in a single layer.
6. Air fry for 10-12 minutes, turning halfway through, until the lamb is cooked to your desired level of doneness.
7. Serve with lemon wedges.

Servings: 4 | **Prep time:** 15 minutes | **Cooking time:** 10-12 minutes

Nutritional info : Calories: 250, Protein: 22g, Fat: 17g, Carbohydrates: 5g, Sugar: 2g

Quick tips:

- Soak wooden skewers in water for at least 30 minutes to prevent burning.
- For extra tenderness, marinate the lamb in the spice mixture for a few hours before cooking.

Rosemary Garlic Lamb Shoulder is a savory and aromatic dish with the rich flavors of rosemary and garlic. The air fryer brings out the best in this cut of lamb, creating a succulent and delicious meal.

Tools needed:

- Ninja Air Fryer Pro
- Mixing bowls
- Air fryer basket
- Cooking spray

Ingredients:

- 2 pounds lamb shoulder, trimmed
- 3 tablespoons olive oil
- 4 cloves garlic, minced
- 2 tablespoons fresh rosemary, chopped
- 1 teaspoon dried thyme
- Salt and pepper to taste

Direction:

1. Preheat the air fryer to 375°F (190°C).
2. In a bowl, mix olive oil, garlic, rosemary, thyme, salt, and pepper.
3. Rub the mixture all over the lamb shoulder.
4. Spray the air fryer basket with cooking spray and place the lamb shoulder in it.
5. Air fry for 25-30 minutes, turning halfway through, until the lamb is cooked through and has a crispy exterior.
6. Let the lamb rest for 10 minutes before slicing.

Servings: 6 | **Prep time:** 10 minutes | **Cooking time:** 25-30 minutes

Nutritional info (per serving, 4 oz):
Calories: 300
Protein: 27g
Fat: 20g
Carbohydrates: 2g
Sugar: 1g

Quick tips:

- Use a meat thermometer to check for doneness; the internal temperature should reach 145°F (63°C) for medium-rare.
- Let the lamb rest before slicing to retain its juices.

Air Fried Lamb Meatballs are tender and flavorful, made with ground lamb and seasoned with a mix of spices. Perfect for a quick dinner or as an appetizer, these meatballs are crispy on the outside and juicy on the inside.

Tools needed:

- Ninja Air Fryer Pro
- Mixing bowls
- Air fryer basket
- Cooking spray

Ingredients:

- 1 pound ground lamb
- 1/2 cup breadcrumbs
- 1/4 cup grated Parmesan cheese
- 1/4 cup fresh mint, chopped
- 2 cloves garlic, minced
- 1 teaspoon ground cumin
- 1 teaspoon smoked paprika
- 1/2 teaspoon ground coriander
- Salt and pepper to taste
- 1 egg, beaten

Direction:

1. Preheat the air fryer to 400°F (200°C).
2. In a bowl, combine ground lamb, breadcrumbs, Parmesan cheese, mint, garlic, cumin, paprika, coriander, salt, pepper, and beaten egg.
3. Mix until well combined and form into 1-inch meatballs.
4. Spray the air fryer basket with cooking spray and arrange the meatballs in a single layer.
5. Air fry for 10-12 minutes, shaking the basket halfway through, until the meatballs are golden brown and cooked through.
6. Serve with a side of tzatziki sauce or over a bed of rice.

Servings: 4 | **Prep time:** 15 minutes | **Cooking time:** 10-12 minutes

Nutritional info (per serving, 4 meatballs): Calories: 220, Protein: 20g, Fat: 14g, Carbohydrates: 8g, Sugar: 2g

Quick tips:

- Avoid overcrowding the basket to ensure even cooking.
- For extra flavor, try adding a pinch of red pepper flakes or a dash of lemon zest to the meatball mixture.

Lamb and Feta Stuffed Bell Peppers are a delicious and hearty dish featuring tender bell peppers filled with a savory mixture of ground lamb, feta cheese, and Mediterranean spices. Perfect for a satisfying meal that's both flavorful and healthy.

Tools needed:

- Ninja Air Fryer Pro
- Mixing bowls
- Air fryer basket
- Cooking spray

Ingredients:

- 4 large bell peppers (any color)
- 1 pound ground lamb
- 1/2 cup crumbled feta cheese
- 1/4 cup fresh parsley, chopped
- 1/4 cup fresh mint, chopped
- 1/2 cup cooked quinoa or rice
- 1 small onion, finely chopped
- 2 cloves garlic, minced
- 1 teaspoon ground cumin
- 1 teaspoon dried oregano
- Salt and pepper to taste
- 1 tablespoon olive oil

Direction:

1. Preheat the air fryer to 375°F (190°C).
2. Cut the tops off the bell peppers and remove the seeds and membranes.
3. In a bowl, mix ground lamb, crumbled feta cheese, parsley, mint, cooked quinoa or rice, onion, garlic, cumin, oregano, salt, pepper, and olive oil until well combined.
4. Stuff the bell peppers with the lamb mixture.
5. Spray the air fryer basket with cooking spray and place the stuffed peppers in it.
6. Air fry for 15-18 minutes, or until the peppers are tender and the lamb is cooked through.
7. Serve warm.

Servings: 4 | **Prep time:** 15 minutes | **Cooking time:** 15-18 minutes

Nutritional info (per serving, 1 stuffed pepper): Calories: 280, Protein: 20g, Fat: 18g, Carbohydrates: 15g, Sugar: 7g

Quick tips:

- To ensure the peppers cook evenly, choose peppers of similar size.
- You can prepare the stuffing mixture a day ahead and refrigerate it for quicker assembly.

Crispy Air Fryer Lamb Ribs are a flavorful and easy-to-make dish with a crispy exterior and tender, juicy meat. Perfect for a quick and indulgent meal or as a standout appetizer.

Tools needed:

- Ninja Air Fryer Pro
- Mixing bowls
- Air fryer basket
- Cooking spray

Ingredients:

- 1 pound lamb ribs
- 2 tablespoons olive oil
- 1 tablespoon smoked paprika
- 1 teaspoon garlic powder
- 1 teaspoon onion powder
- 1 teaspoon ground cumin
- 1/2 teaspoon dried thyme
- Salt and pepper to taste

Direction:

1. Preheat the air fryer to 400°F (200°C).
2. In a bowl, mix olive oil, smoked paprika, garlic powder, onion powder, cumin, thyme, salt, and pepper.
3. Rub the spice mixture all over the lamb ribs.
4. Spray the air fryer basket with cooking spray and place the lamb ribs in a single layer.
5. Air fry for 15-20 minutes, turning halfway through, until the ribs are crispy and cooked through.
6. Let the ribs rest for a few minutes before cutting between the bones.

Servings: 4 | **Prep time:** 10 minutes | **Cooking time:** 15-20 minutes

Nutritional info (per serving, 4 ribs):
Calories: 320
Protein: 25g
Fat: 22g
Carbohydrates: 5g
Sugar: 1g

Quick tips:

- Ensure the ribs are arranged in a single layer for even cooking.
- For extra crispiness, you can increase the cooking time slightly, but monitor closely to avoid burning.

Mint Crusted Lamb Cutlets

Mint Crusted Lamb Cutlets are elegant and full of flavor, featuring a crispy mint and herb crust that pairs beautifully with the tender lamb. An excellent choice for a special dinner or festive occasion.

Tools needed:

- Ninja Air Fryer Pro
- Mixing bowls
- Air fryer basket
- Cooking spray

Ingredients:

- 8 lamb cutlets
- 1 cup fresh mint leaves, chopped
- 1/2 cup fresh parsley, chopped
- 1/2 cup breadcrumbs
- 1/4 cup grated Parmesan cheese
- 2 cloves garlic, minced
- 1 tablespoon Dijon mustard
- Salt and pepper to taste
- 1 egg, beaten

Direction:

1. Preheat the air fryer to 400°F (200°C).
2. In a bowl, combine mint leaves, parsley, breadcrumbs, Parmesan cheese, garlic, salt, and pepper.
3. Brush each lamb cutlet with Dijon mustard and dip into the beaten egg, then coat with the mint mixture.
4. Spray the air fryer basket with cooking spray and arrange the cutlets in a single layer.
5. Air fry for 8-10 minutes, turning halfway through, until the crust is crispy and the lamb is cooked to your desired doneness.
6. Serve with a side of mint yogurt sauce or your favorite vegetables.

Servings: 4 | **Prep time:** 15 minutes | **Cooking time:** 8-10 minutes

Nutritional info (per serving, 2 cutlets): Calories: 290, Protein: 25g, Fat: 20g, Carbohydrates: 12g, Sugar: 2g

Quick tips:

- For an even coating, ensure the lamb cutlets are well-dried before applying the mustard.
- Let the cutlets rest for a few minutes after cooking to allow the juices to redistribute.

Air Fried Lamb Shawarma brings the savory and aromatic flavors of Middle Eastern cuisine right to your kitchen. Marinated in a blend of spices and cooked to perfection, this dish is both easy and delicious, perfect for a quick weeknight meal or a flavorful wrap.

Tools needed:

- Ninja Air Fryer Pro
- Mixing bowls
- Air fryer basket
- Cooking spray

Ingredients:

- 1 pound lamb, thinly sliced (shoulder or leg)
- 2 tablespoons olive oil
- 2 tablespoons shawarma seasoning (or a mix of cumin, coriander, paprika, turmeric, and garlic powder)
- 1 tablespoon lemon juice
- 3 cloves garlic, minced
- 1 teaspoon ground cinnamon
- Salt and pepper to taste

Direction:

1. Preheat the air fryer to 400°F (200°C).
2. In a bowl, combine olive oil, shawarma seasoning, lemon juice, garlic, cinnamon, salt, and pepper.
3. Toss the lamb slices in the marinade until well coated. Let marinate for at least 30 minutes (or up to 4 hours in the refrigerator).
4. Spray the air fryer basket with cooking spray and place the marinated lamb slices in a single layer.
5. Air fry for 10-12 minutes, shaking the basket halfway through, until the lamb is crispy and cooked through.
6. Serve with pita bread, hummus, and your favorite toppings like cucumber, tomato, and tahini sauce.

Servings: 4 | **Prep time:** 10 minutes | **Cooking time:** 10-12 minutes

Nutritional info (per serving, 1/4 of recipe): Calories: 270, Protein: 22g, Fat: 19g, Carbohydrates: 4g, Sugar: 1g

Quick tips:

- For a more authentic taste, serve with a side of garlic sauce or a fresh salad.
- Ensure the lamb slices are not overcrowded in the air fryer for even cooking.

Lamb and Chickpea Patties

Lamb and Chickpea Patties are hearty and flavorful, combining ground lamb with chickpeas and spices to create delicious patties that are perfect for a quick meal or as an appetizer. The air fryer gives them a crispy exterior without excess oil.

Tools needed:

- Ninja Air Fryer Pro
- Mixing bowls
- Air fryer basket
- Cooking spray

Ingredients:

- 1 pound ground lamb
- 1 cup canned chickpeas, drained and rinsed
- 1/2 cup breadcrumbs
- 1/4 cup fresh parsley, chopped
- 1/4 cup fresh cilantro, chopped
- 1 small onion, finely chopped
- 2 cloves garlic, minced
- 1 teaspoon ground cumin
- 1 teaspoon ground coriander
- 1/2 teaspoon paprika
- Salt and pepper to taste
- 1 egg, beaten

Direction:

1. Preheat the air fryer to 400°F (200°C).
2. In a food processor, pulse the chickpeas until coarsely chopped.
3. In a bowl, combine ground lamb, chickpeas, breadcrumbs, parsley, cilantro, onion, garlic, cumin, coriander, paprika, salt, pepper, and beaten egg. Mix well.
4. Form the mixture into 1-inch patties.
5. Spray the air fryer basket with cooking spray and arrange the patties in a single layer.
6. Air fry for 8-10 minutes, turning halfway through, until the patties are golden brown and cooked through.
7. Serve with a side of yogurt sauce or in a pita with fresh vegetables.

Servings: 4 | **Prep time:** 15 minutes | **Cooking time:** 8-10 minutes

Nutritional info (per serving, 3 patties): Calories: 280, Protein: 22g, Fat: 14g, Carbohydrates: 19g, Sugar: 2g

Quick tips:

- Use a food processor for an even texture in the patties.
- For extra crispiness, lightly spray the patties with cooking spray before air frying.

Moroccan Spiced Air Fryer Lamb is infused with rich and aromatic spices typical of Moroccan cuisine. This dish offers a deliciously spiced and tender lamb that's perfect for a flavorful dinner or a special occasion.

Tools needed:

- Ninja Air Fryer Pro
- Mixing bowls
- Air fryer basket
- Cooking spray

Ingredients:

- 1 pound lamb chops or shoulder, cut into chunks
- 2 tablespoons olive oil
- 2 tablespoons Moroccan spice blend (or a mix of paprika, cumin, coriander, cinnamon, ginger, and turmeric)
- 3 cloves garlic, minced
- 1 tablespoon honey
- 1 tablespoon lemon juice
- Salt and pepper to taste

Direction:

1. Preheat the air fryer to 400°F (200°C).
2. In a bowl, mix olive oil, Moroccan spice blend, garlic, honey, lemon juice, salt, and pepper.
3. Toss the lamb pieces in the spice mixture until well coated.
4. Spray the air fryer basket with cooking spray and arrange the lamb in a single layer.
5. Air fry for 12-15 minutes, turning halfway through, until the lamb is tender and slightly crispy on the outside.
6. Serve with couscous or a side salad.

Servings: 4 | **Prep time:** 10 minutes | **Cooking time:** 12-15 minutes

Nutritional info (per serving, 4 oz):
Calories: 300
Protein: 23g
Fat: 20g
Carbohydrates: 10g
Sugar: 6g

Quick tips:

- For a deeper flavor, marinate the lamb in the spice mixture for a few hours before cooking.
- Serve with a side of mint yogurt sauce to complement the Moroccan spices.

AIRFRYER APPETIZERS & SNACKS

Air Fryer Mozzarella Sticks

Air Fryer Mozzarella Sticks are a perfect snack or appetizer with a gooey, cheesy center and a crispy, golden exterior. Made with minimal oil, they're a healthier alternative to traditional fried mozzarella sticks but still packed with flavor.

Tools needed:

- Ninja Air Fryer Pro
- Mixing bowls
- Air fryer basket
- Cooking spray
- Toothpicks or skewers (optional)

Ingredients:

- 12 mozzarella string cheese sticks
- 1/2 cup all-purpose flour
- 2 large eggs, beaten
- 1 cup breadcrumbs
- 1/2 cup grated Parmesan cheese
- 1 teaspoon dried Italian seasoning
- Salt and pepper to taste
- Cooking spray

Direction:

1. Preheat the air fryer to 390°F (200°C).
2. Set up a breading station: Place flour in one bowl, beaten eggs in another, and a mixture of breadcrumbs, Parmesan cheese, Italian seasoning, salt, and pepper in a third bowl.
3. Dredge each mozzarella stick in flour, then dip into the beaten eggs, and finally coat with the breadcrumb mixture. Press the breadcrumbs firmly onto the cheese to ensure they stick.
4. Place the breaded mozzarella sticks on a plate and freeze for 30 minutes to an hour.
5. Spray the air fryer basket with cooking spray and arrange the frozen mozzarella sticks in a single layer.
6. Air fry for 6-8 minutes, or until golden brown and crispy.
7. Serve warm with marinara sauce for dipping.

Servings: 4 | **Prep time:** 10 minutes | **Cooking time:** 6-8 minutes

Nutritional info : Calories: 300, Protein: 16g, Fat: 20g, Carbohydrates: 20g, Sugar: 2g
Quick tips:

- Freezing the mozzarella sticks before air frying helps prevent the cheese from melting too quickly and oozing out.
- Serve immediately for the best texture.

Crispy Air Fried Zucchini Chips are a crunchy, low-carb snack that's a great alternative to traditional potato chips. They're seasoned to perfection and perfect for dipping or enjoying on their own.

Tools needed:

- Ninja Air Fryer Pro
- Mandoline or knife
- Mixing bowls
- Air fryer basket
- Cooking spray

Ingredients:

- 2 medium zucchinis, sliced into thin rounds
- 1/2 cup all-purpose flour
- 2 large eggs, beaten
- 1 cup panko breadcrumbs
- 1/2 cup grated Parmesan cheese
- 1 teaspoon garlic powder
- 1 teaspoon dried oregano
- Salt and pepper to taste
- Cooking spray

Direction:

1. Preheat the air fryer to 400°F (200°C).
2. In a bowl, toss zucchini slices with flour to coat.
3. Dip each zucchini slice into the beaten eggs, then coat with a mixture of panko breadcrumbs, Parmesan cheese, garlic powder, oregano, salt, and pepper.
4. Spray the air fryer basket with cooking spray and arrange the coated zucchini slices in a single layer.
5. Air fry for 8-10 minutes, shaking the basket halfway through, until the zucchini chips are crispy and golden brown.
6. Serve with your favorite dipping sauce or as a crunchy snack.

Servings: 4 | **Prep time:** 15 minutes | **Cooking time:** 8-10 minutes

Nutritional info (per serving, 1 cup of chips): Calories: 150, Protein: 6g, Fat: 8g, Carbohydrates: 18g, Sugar: 4g

Quick tips:

- Slice the zucchini as uniformly as possible for even cooking.
- For extra crispiness, you can add a light spray of cooking oil on the chips before air frying.

Buffalo Cauliflower Bites

Buffalo Cauliflower Bites are a spicy and tangy alternative to traditional buffalo wings. They're crispy on the outside and tender on the inside, making them a great choice for a healthy snack or appetizer with a kick.

Tools needed:

- Ninja Air Fryer Pro
- Mixing bowls
- Air fryer basket
- Cooking spray

Ingredients:

- 1 large head of cauliflower, cut into bite-sized florets
- 1 cup all-purpose flour
- 1/2 cup milk or dairy-free milk
- 1 teaspoon garlic powder
- 1 teaspoon onion powder
- 1 teaspoon paprika
- Salt and pepper to taste
- 1 cup buffalo sauce
- 2 tablespoons olive oil

Direction:

1. Preheat the air fryer to 400°F (200°C).
2. In a bowl, whisk together flour, milk, garlic powder, onion powder, paprika, salt, and pepper to create a batter.
3. Toss the cauliflower florets in the batter until fully coated.
4. Spray the air fryer basket with cooking spray and arrange the battered cauliflower in a single layer.
5. Air fry for 12-15 minutes, shaking the basket halfway through, until the cauliflower is crispy and golden.
6. Toss the crispy cauliflower in buffalo sauce and return to the air fryer for an additional 2-3 minutes to set the sauce.
7. Serve with celery sticks and ranch or blue cheese dressing.

Servings: 4 | **Prep time:** 15 minutes | **Cooking time:** 12-15 minutes

Nutritional info (per serving, 1 cup): Calories: 180, Protein: 5g, Fat: 10g, Carbohydrates: 22g, Sugar: 4g

Quick tips:

- For less mess, toss the cauliflower in the buffalo sauce directly in the air fryer basket after cooking.
- Adjust the amount of buffalo sauce to suit your preferred level of heat.

Air Fryer Onion Rings are a classic favorite with a crispy coating and tender, sweet onions inside. Made in the air fryer, these rings offer a healthier alternative to deep-frying while still delivering a satisfying crunch.

Tools needed:

- Ninja Air Fryer Pro
- Mixing bowls
- Air fryer basket
- Cooking spray
- Baking sheet (optional)

Ingredients:

- 2 large onions, sliced into 1/4-inch rings
- 1 cup all-purpose flour
- 2 large eggs, beaten
- 1 cup panko breadcrumbs
- 1/2 cup grated Parmesan cheese
- 1 teaspoon paprika
- 1 teaspoon garlic powder
- Salt and pepper to taste
- Cooking spray

Direction:

1. Preheat the air fryer to 400°F (200°C).
2. Set up a breading station: Place flour in one bowl, beaten eggs in another, and a mixture of panko breadcrumbs, Parmesan cheese, paprika, garlic powder, salt, and pepper in a third bowl.
3. Dredge each onion ring in flour, then dip into the beaten eggs, and coat with the breadcrumb mixture. Press the breadcrumbs firmly onto the onion rings.
4. Spray the air fryer basket with cooking spray and arrange the onion rings in a single layer. You may need to cook in batches.
5. Air fry for 8-10 minutes, flipping halfway through, until golden brown and crispy.
6. Serve with ketchup or your favorite dipping sauce.

Servings: 4 | **Prep time:** 15 minutes | **Cooking time:** 8-10 minutes per batch

Nutritional info (per serving, 4 rings): Calories: 250, Protein: 6g, Fat: 12g, Carbohydrates: 31g, Sugar: 6g

Quick tips:

- For extra crispiness, lightly spray the onion rings with cooking spray before air frying.
- Avoid overcrowding the basket to ensure even cooking.

Spicy Air Fried Jalapeno Poppers

Spicy Air Fried Jalapeno Poppers are a bold and flavorful appetizer with a creamy cheese filling and a crispy coating. The air fryer makes them healthier by reducing the amount of oil needed, while still achieving that perfect crunch.

Tools needed:

- Ninja Air Fryer Pro
- Mixing bowls
- Air fryer basket
- Cooking spray

Ingredients:

- 12 fresh jalapenos, halved and seeded
- 4 ounces cream cheese, softened
- 1/2 cup shredded cheddar cheese
- 1/4 cup grated Parmesan cheese
- 1/2 teaspoon garlic powder
- 1/2 teaspoon smoked paprika
- 1/2 cup all-purpose flour
- 1 large egg, beaten
- 1 cup panko breadcrumbs
- Cooking spray

Direction:

1. Preheat the air fryer to 370°F (190°C).
2. In a bowl, mix cream cheese, cheddar cheese, Parmesan cheese, garlic powder, and smoked paprika until well combined.
3. Spoon the cheese mixture into the jalapeno halves.
4. Set up a breading station: Place flour in one bowl, beaten egg in another, and panko breadcrumbs in a third bowl.
5. Dredge each stuffed jalapeno in flour, dip in the beaten egg, and coat with breadcrumbs.
6. Spray the air fryer basket with cooking spray and arrange the jalapeno poppers in a single layer.
7. Air fry for 8-10 minutes, or until the cheese is melted and the breadcrumbs are golden brown.
8. Serve warm.

Servings: 4 | **Prep time:** 15 minutes | **Cooking time:** 8-10 minutes

Nutritional info : Calories: 300, Protein: 10g, Fat: 25g, Carbohydrates: 15g, Sugar: 4g
Quick tips:

- For a milder version, remove all seeds and membranes from the jalapenos.
- Serve with a side of ranch or blue cheese dressing for dipping.

Air Fried Pretzel Bites are a delightful snack with a soft, chewy center and a golden-brown, salty crust. These bite-sized treats are perfect for game day or as a fun appetizer, and they're made even better with a quick dip in mustard or cheese sauce.

Tools needed:

- Ninja Air Fryer Pro
- Mixing bowls
- Air fryer basket
- Rolling pin
- Cooking spray
- Pastry brush

Ingredients:

- 1 can (12 oz) refrigerated pizza dough
- 1/4 cup baking soda
- 1 cup warm water
- Coarse sea salt
- 2 tablespoons melted butter
- Cooking spray

Direction:

1. Preheat the air fryer to 370°F (190°C).
2. In a bowl, mix baking soda with warm water to create a solution.
3. Roll out the pizza dough on a lightly floured surface and cut into 1-inch pieces.
4. Dip each dough piece into the baking soda solution, then place on a paper towel to drain.
5. Spray the air fryer basket with cooking spray and arrange the pretzel bites in a single layer.
6. Air fry for 6-8 minutes, or until golden brown.
7. Brush with melted butter and sprinkle with coarse sea salt before serving.

Servings: 4 | **Prep time:** 10 minutes | **Cooking time:** 6-8 minutes

Nutritional info (per serving, 8 pretzel bites):
Calories: 220
Protein: 6g
Fat: 9g
Carbohydrates: 28g
Sugar: 1g

Quick tips:

- Make sure to not overcrowd the basket to ensure each pretzel bite gets crispy.
- Serve with mustard, cheese sauce, or your favorite dip for added flavor.

Air Fryer Stuffed Mushrooms

Air Fryer Stuffed Mushrooms are a savory and satisfying appetizer with a deliciously cheesy filling. They're easy to prepare and cook quickly in the air fryer, making them a perfect choice for a party or a quick snack.

Tools needed:

- Ninja Air Fryer Pro
- Mixing bowls
- Air fryer basket
- Cooking spray

Ingredients:

- 12 large mushrooms, stems removed
- 1/2 cup cream cheese, softened
- 1/4 cup grated Parmesan cheese
- 1/4 cup shredded mozzarella cheese
- 2 tablespoons finely chopped fresh parsley
- 2 cloves garlic, minced
- 1/4 teaspoon dried thyme
- Salt and pepper to taste
- Cooking spray

Direction:

1. Preheat the air fryer to 370°F (190°C).
2. In a bowl, mix cream cheese, Parmesan cheese, mozzarella cheese, parsley, garlic, thyme, salt, and pepper until well combined.
3. Spoon the cheese mixture into the mushroom caps, packing it in firmly.
4. Spray the air fryer basket with cooking spray and arrange the stuffed mushrooms in a single layer.
5. Air fry for 8-10 minutes, or until the mushrooms are tender and the topping is golden brown.
6. Serve warm.

Servings: 4 | **Prep time:** 15 minutes | **Cooking time:** 8-10 minutes

Nutritional info (per serving, 3 mushrooms): Calories: 150, Protein: 8g, Fat: 11g, Carbohydrates: 7g, Sugar: 2g

Quick tips:

- For extra flavor, add a pinch of red pepper flakes to the cheese mixture.
- If you have extra filling, you can use it to stuff other vegetables or even as a spread on bread.

Garlic Parmesan Air Fryer Fries are a crispy, flavorful alternative to regular fries. Tossed in garlic and Parmesan cheese, these fries are perfect as a side dish or a standalone snack, and they're made healthier with the air fryer.

Tools needed:

- Ninja Air Fryer Pro
- Mixing bowls
- Air fryer basket
- Cooking spray

Ingredients:

- 4 large russet potatoes, peeled and cut into fries
- 2 tablespoons olive oil
- 1 teaspoon garlic powder
- 1/2 cup grated Parmesan cheese
- 1 teaspoon dried Italian seasoning
- Salt and pepper to taste
- Cooking spray

Direction:

1. Preheat the air fryer to 400°F (200°C).
2. In a bowl, toss the potato fries with olive oil, garlic powder, salt, and pepper until evenly coated.
3. Spray the air fryer basket with cooking spray and arrange the fries in a single layer.
4. Air fry for 15-18 minutes, shaking the basket halfway through, until crispy and golden brown.
5. Remove from the air fryer and immediately toss with Parmesan cheese and Italian seasoning.
6. Serve warm.

Servings: 4 | **Prep time:** 10 minutes | **Cooking time:** 15-18 minutes

Nutritional info (per serving, 1 cup fries):
Calories: 220
Protein: 6g
Fat: 12g
Carbohydrates: 24g
Sugar: 2g

Quick tips:

- For crispier fries, soak the cut potatoes in cold water for at least 30 minutes before cooking to remove excess starch.
- Adjust the amount of garlic powder and Parmesan to taste.

Air Fried Chicken Wontons are a crispy and delicious appetizer or snack with a savory chicken filling. The air fryer provides a crispy texture without the need for deep frying, making these wontons a healthier choice.

Tools needed:

- Ninja Air Fryer Pro
- Mixing bowls
- Air fryer basket
- Cooking spray

Ingredients:

- 1 cup cooked chicken, shredded
- 1/2 cup cream cheese, softened
- 1/4 cup finely chopped green onions
- 2 cloves garlic, minced
- 1 tablespoon soy sauce
- 1/2 teaspoon ginger, minced
- 12 wonton wrappers
- Cooking spray

Direction:

1. Preheat the air fryer to 375°F (190°C).
2. In a bowl, mix cooked chicken, cream cheese, green onions, garlic, soy sauce, and ginger until well combined.
3. Place a small spoonful of the filling in the center of each wonton wrapper. Moisten the edges with water and fold into a triangle or pleat the edges to seal.
4. Spray the air fryer basket with cooking spray and arrange the wontons in a single layer.
5. Air fry for 6-8 minutes, or until golden brown and crispy.
6. Serve warm with sweet and sour sauce or soy sauce for dipping.

Servings: 4 | **Prep time:** 15 minutes | **Cooking time:** 6-8 minutes

Nutritional info (per serving, 3 wontons):
Calories: 180
Protein: 10g
Fat: 10g
Carbohydrates: 14g
Sugar: 1g

Quick tips:

- Be sure to seal the wontons completely to avoid any filling leaking out during cooking.
- Serve with a side of dipping sauce to enhance the flavor.

BBQ Air Fryer Tofu Bites

BBQ Air Fryer Tofu Bites are a delicious and healthy plant-based alternative to traditional BBQ snacks. With a crispy exterior and smoky BBQ flavor, these tofu bites make a satisfying appetizer or main dish.

Tools needed:

- Ninja Air Fryer Pro
- Mixing bowls
- Air fryer basket
- Cooking spray

Ingredients:

- 1 block (14 oz) firm tofu, drained and pressed
- 1/2 cup BBQ sauce (store-bought or homemade)
- 1/4 cup cornstarch
- 1 tablespoon olive oil
- 1 teaspoon smoked paprika
- Salt and pepper to taste
- Cooking spray

Direction:

1. Preheat the air fryer to 400°F (200°C).
2. Cut the tofu into 1-inch cubes.
3. In a bowl, toss the tofu cubes with cornstarch until evenly coated.
4. Drizzle with olive oil and toss to coat. Season with smoked paprika, salt, and pepper.
5. Spray the air fryer basket with cooking spray and arrange the tofu cubes in a single layer.
6. Air fry for 12-15 minutes, shaking the basket halfway through, until golden and crispy.
7. Remove the tofu from the air fryer and toss with BBQ sauce.
8. Serve warm.

Servings: 4 | **Prep time:** 15 minutes | **Cooking time:** 12-15 minutes

Nutritional info (per serving, 1/4 of recipe):
Calories: 220
Protein: 15g
Fat: 10g
Carbohydrates: 20g
Sugar: 8g

Quick tips:

- Ensure the tofu is well-pressed to remove excess moisture for a crispier texture.
- For extra flavor, marinate the tofu in BBQ sauce for 30 minutes before air frying.

AIRFRYER FISH & SEAFOOD RECIPES

Air Fryer Coconut Shrimp

Air Fryer Coconut Shrimp are a delightful appetizer with a crispy, golden coating and a hint of tropical coconut flavor. The air fryer provides a healthier take on this classic dish without sacrificing crunch.

Tools needed:

- Ninja Air Fryer Pro
- Mixing bowls
- Air fryer basket
- Cooking spray

Ingredients:

- 1 pound large shrimp, peeled and deveined
- 1/2 cup all-purpose flour
- 1/2 cup shredded coconut
- 1/2 cup panko breadcrumbs
- 2 large eggs, beaten
- 1/2 teaspoon paprika
- Salt and pepper to taste
- Cooking spray

Direction:

1. Preheat the air fryer to 370°F (190°C).
2. Set up a breading station: Place flour in one bowl, beaten eggs in another, and a mixture of shredded coconut, panko breadcrumbs, paprika, salt, and pepper in a third bowl.
3. Dredge each shrimp in flour, dip in the beaten eggs, and coat with the coconut breadcrumb mixture.
4. Spray the air fryer basket with cooking spray and arrange the shrimp in a single layer.
5. Air fry for 6-8 minutes, or until golden brown and crispy.
6. Serve with a side of sweet chili sauce or your favorite dipping sauce.

Servings: 4 | **Prep time:** 15 minutes | **Cooking time:** 6-8 minutes

Nutritional info (per serving, 6 shrimp): Calories: 240, Protein: 18g, Fat: 10g, Carbohydrates: 20g, Sugar: 5g

Quick tips:

- For a lighter coating, use unsweetened shredded coconut.
- If using large shrimp, you may need to adjust the cooking time slightly.

Crispy Air Fried Fish Tacos are a delicious and healthy twist on a classic favorite. With crispy fish fillets and fresh toppings, these tacos are perfect for a light lunch or dinner.

Tools needed:

- Ninja Air Fryer Pro
- Mixing bowls
- Air fryer basket
- Cooking spray
- Small tortillas

Ingredients:

- 1 pound white fish fillets (such as cod or tilapia), cut into strips
- 1/2 cup all-purpose flour
- 1/2 cup cornmeal
- 1/2 cup panko breadcrumbs
- 2 large eggs, beaten
- 1 teaspoon paprika
- 1/2 teaspoon garlic powder
- Salt and pepper to taste
- Cooking spray
- Small tortillas
- Shredded cabbage, for serving
- Lime wedges, for serving

Direction:

1. Preheat the air fryer to 400°F (200°C).
2. Set up a breading station: Place flour in one bowl, beaten eggs in another, and a mixture of cornmeal, panko breadcrumbs, paprika, garlic powder, salt, and pepper in a third bowl.
3. Dredge each fish strip in flour, dip in the beaten eggs, and coat with the breadcrumb mixture.
4. Spray the air fryer basket with cooking spray and arrange the fish strips in a single layer.
5. Air fry for 8-10 minutes, flipping halfway through, until golden brown and crispy.
6. Serve the fish strips in tortillas with shredded cabbage and lime wedges.

Servings: 4 | **Prep time:** 15 minutes | **Cooking time:** 8-10 minutes

Nutritional info : Calories: 320, Protein: 20g, Fat: 10g, Carbohydrates: 30g, Sugar: 3g
Quick tips:

- For added flavor, season the fish fillets with a bit of chili powder or cumin before breading.
- Use a slaw mix or your favorite taco toppings for extra crunch and flavor.

Lemon Butter Air Fryer Salmon

Lemon Butter Air Fryer Salmon offers a delectable blend of buttery, zesty flavors with a perfectly crispy exterior. This dish is quick and easy to prepare, making it an ideal choice for a healthy weeknight dinner.

Tools needed:

- Ninja Air Fryer Pro
- Mixing bowls
- Air fryer basket
- Cooking spray

Ingredients:

- 4 salmon fillets (about 6 oz each)
- 2 tablespoons melted butter
- 1 lemon, zest and juice
- 2 cloves garlic, minced
- 1 teaspoon dried dill
- Salt and pepper to taste
- Fresh parsley, chopped (for garnish)
- Cooking spray

Direction:

1. Preheat the air fryer to 400°F (200°C).
2. In a small bowl, mix melted butter, lemon zest, lemon juice, garlic, dill, salt, and pepper.
3. Brush the salmon fillets with the lemon butter mixture.
4. Spray the air fryer basket with cooking spray and place the salmon fillets in a single layer.
5. Air fry for 8-10 minutes, or until the salmon is cooked through and flakes easily with a fork.
6. Garnish with fresh parsley and serve warm.

Servings: 4 | **Prep time:** 10 minutes | **Cooking time:** 8-10 minutes

Nutritional info (per serving):
Calories: 320
Protein: 27g
Fat: 22g
Carbohydrates: 3g
Sugar: 1g

Quick tips:

- For a crispier skin, place the salmon skin-side down in the air fryer.
- Adjust the cooking time depending on the thickness of the salmon fillets.

Air Fried Calamari is a healthier take on this classic appetizer, offering a crispy texture and light, savory flavor without the need for deep frying. It's perfect for serving as a snack or appetizer at gatherings.

Tools needed:

- Ninja Air Fryer Pro
- Mixing bowls
- Air fryer basket
- Cooking spray

Ingredients:

- 1 pound calamari rings (fresh or thawed)
- 1/2 cup all-purpose flour
- 1/2 cup cornmeal
- 1/2 cup panko breadcrumbs
- 1 teaspoon paprika
- 1/2 teaspoon garlic powder
- Salt and pepper to taste
- 2 large eggs, beaten
- Cooking spray
- Lemon wedges (for serving)

Direction:

1. Preheat the air fryer to 400°F (200°C).
2. Set up a breading station: Place flour in one bowl, beaten eggs in another, and a mixture of cornmeal, panko breadcrumbs, paprika, garlic powder, salt, and pepper in a third bowl.
3. Dredge each calamari ring in flour, dip in the beaten eggs, and coat with the breadcrumb mixture.
4. Spray the air fryer basket with cooking spray and arrange the calamari rings in a single layer.
5. Air fry for 6-8 minutes, shaking the basket halfway through, until golden and crispy.
6. Serve with lemon wedges for a zesty touch.

Servings: 4 | **Prep time:** 15 minutes | **Cooking time:** 6-8 minutes

Nutritional info (per serving, 6-8 rings): Calories: 230, Protein: 12g, Fat: 10g, Carbohydrates: 24g, Sugar: 1g

Quick tips:

- Avoid overcrowding the air fryer basket to ensure even cooking and crispiness.
- Serve with a side of marinara sauce or aioli for dipping.

Garlic Herb Air Fryer Scallops

Garlic Herb Air Fryer Scallops are a flavorful and elegant dish, perfect for a special occasion or a sophisticated weeknight meal. The air fryer ensures they are perfectly cooked with a tender interior and a light, crispy exterior.

Tools needed:

- Ninja Air Fryer Pro
- Mixing bowls
- Air fryer basket
- Cooking spray

Ingredients:

- 1 pound large sea scallops, patted dry
- 2 tablespoons olive oil
- 3 cloves garlic, minced
- 1 tablespoon fresh thyme leaves
- 1 tablespoon fresh parsley, chopped
- Salt and pepper to taste
- Lemon wedges (for serving)
- Cooking spray

Direction:

1. Preheat the air fryer to 400°F (200°C).
2. In a bowl, toss the scallops with olive oil, garlic, thyme, parsley, salt, and pepper.
3. Spray the air fryer basket with cooking spray and arrange the scallops in a single layer.
4. Air fry for 6-8 minutes, flipping halfway through, until the scallops are opaque and cooked through.
5. Serve with lemon wedges.

Servings: 4 | **Prep time:** 10 minutes | **Cooking time:** 6-8 minutes

Nutritional info (per serving, 4 scallops):
Calories: 200
Protein: 25g
Fat: 10g
Carbohydrates: 2g
Sugar: 1g

Quick tips:

- Ensure scallops are dry before seasoning to achieve a better sear.
- For extra flavor, you can add a sprinkle of Parmesan cheese before air frying.

Spicy Air Fryer Fish Fillets are a zesty and healthy option for fish lovers. With a crispy coating and a kick of heat, these fillets are perfect for a quick weeknight dinner or a flavorful lunch.

Tools needed:

- Ninja Air Fryer Pro
- Mixing bowls
- Air fryer basket
- Cooking spray

Ingredients:

- 4 fish fillets (such as tilapia or cod)
- 1/2 cup all-purpose flour
- 1/2 cup cornmeal
- 1/2 cup panko breadcrumbs
- 1 tablespoon chili powder
- 1 teaspoon cayenne pepper (adjust to taste)
- 1 teaspoon paprika
- 1 teaspoon garlic powder
- Salt and pepper to taste
- 2 large eggs, beaten
- Cooking spray

Direction:

1. Preheat the air fryer to 400°F (200°C).
2. Set up a breading station: Place flour in one bowl, beaten eggs in another, and a mixture of cornmeal, panko breadcrumbs, chili powder, cayenne pepper, paprika, garlic powder, salt, and pepper in a third bowl.
3. Dredge each fish fillet in flour, dip in the beaten eggs, and coat with the breadcrumb mixture.
4. Spray the air fryer basket with cooking spray and place the fish fillets in a single layer.
5. Air fry for 8-10 minutes, or until the fish is golden brown and cooked through, flipping halfway through.
6. Serve with a side of tartar sauce or a fresh salad.

Servings: 4 | **Prep time:** 15 minutes | **Cooking time:** 8-10 minutes

Nutritional info (per serving): Calories: 270, Protein: 24g, Fat: 12g, Carbohydrates: 20g, Sugar: 1g

Quick tips:

- For a milder version, reduce the amount of cayenne pepper.
- Ensure the fish fillets are thoroughly dried before breading to help the coating adhere better.

Air Fried Crab Cakes

Air Fried Crab Cakes are a healthier twist on a classic seafood dish. These cakes are packed with tender crab meat and spices, providing a crispy exterior and a moist interior, all without the need for deep frying.

Tools needed:

- Ninja Air Fryer Pro
- Mixing bowls
- Air fryer basket
- Cooking spray

Ingredients:

- 1 pound lump crab meat
- 1/2 cup breadcrumbs
- 1/4 cup mayonnaise
- 1 large egg
- 1 tablespoon Dijon mustard
- 1 tablespoon fresh parsley, chopped
- 1 teaspoon Old Bay seasoning
- 1/2 teaspoon paprika
- Salt and pepper to taste
- Cooking spray

Direction:

1. Preheat the air fryer to 370°F (190°C).
2. In a bowl, mix crab meat, breadcrumbs, mayonnaise, egg, Dijon mustard, parsley, Old Bay seasoning, paprika, salt, and pepper until well combined.
3. Shape the mixture into 8 small patties.
4. Spray the air fryer basket with cooking spray and arrange the crab cakes in a single layer.
5. Air fry for 8-10 minutes, flipping halfway through, until the cakes are golden brown and crispy.
6. Serve with a side of tartar sauce or a fresh salad.

Servings: 4 | **Prep time:** 15 minutes | **Cooking time:** 8-10 minutes

Nutritional info (per serving, 2 crab cakes): Calories: 250, Protein: 18g, Fat: 15g, Carbohydrates: 10g, Sugar: 2g

Quick tips:

- For best results, use fresh lump crab meat rather than imitation crab.
- Chill the crab cakes in the refrigerator for about 30 minutes before air frying to help them hold their shape.

Honey Sriracha Shrimp are a delightful blend of sweet and spicy flavors, with a crispy texture from the air fryer. This dish makes a great appetizer or main course, combining a touch of honey with the heat of Sriracha for a perfect balance.

Tools needed:

- Ninja Air Fryer Pro
- Mixing bowls
- Air fryer basket
- Cooking spray

Ingredients:

- 1 pound large shrimp, peeled and deveined
- 2 tablespoons honey
- 2 tablespoons Sriracha sauce
- 1 tablespoon soy sauce
- 1 teaspoon minced garlic
- 1 teaspoon grated ginger
- 1 tablespoon olive oil
- Salt and pepper to taste
- Cooking spray

Direction:

1. Preheat the air fryer to 400°F (200°C).
2. In a bowl, mix honey, Sriracha sauce, soy sauce, garlic, ginger, olive oil, salt, and pepper.
3. Toss the shrimp in the sauce mixture until evenly coated.
4. Spray the air fryer basket with cooking spray and arrange the shrimp in a single layer.
5. Air fry for 6-8 minutes, or until the shrimp are cooked through and crispy, shaking the basket halfway through.
6. Serve immediately, garnished with chopped scallions or sesame seeds if desired.

Servings: 4 | **Prep time:** 10 minutes | **Cooking time:** 6-8 minutes

Nutritional info (per serving, 6 shrimp): Calories: 200, Protein: 22g, Fat: 8g, Carbohydrates: 12g, Sugar: 9g

Quick tips:

- Adjust the amount of Sriracha based on your heat preference.
- For a complete meal, serve the shrimp over steamed rice or with a side of sautéed vegetables.

Air Fryer Mahi Mahi is a quick and healthy seafood dish that delivers a tender, flaky texture with a crispy exterior. This recipe is perfect for a light and flavorful dinner, showcasing the air fryer's ability to cook fish to perfection without excessive oil.

Tools needed:

- Ninja Air Fryer Pro
- Mixing bowls
- Air fryer basket
- Cooking spray

Ingredients:

- 4 mahi mahi fillets (about 6 oz each)
- 2 tablespoons olive oil
- 1 teaspoon lemon zest
- 1 tablespoon lemon juice
- 1 teaspoon dried oregano
- 1 teaspoon garlic powder
- 1/2 teaspoon paprika
- Salt and pepper to taste
- Fresh lemon wedges (for serving)
- Cooking spray

Direction:

1. Preheat the air fryer to 400°F (200°C).
2. In a small bowl, mix olive oil, lemon zest, lemon juice, oregano, garlic powder, paprika, salt, and pepper.
3. Brush the mahi mahi fillets with the olive oil mixture.
4. Spray the air fryer basket with cooking spray and place the fillets in a single layer.
5. Air fry for 8-10 minutes, or until the fish is opaque and flakes easily with a fork.
6. Serve with fresh lemon wedges and a side of your choice.

Servings: 4 | **Prep time:** 10 minutes | **Cooking time:** 8-10 minutes

Nutritional info (per serving): Calories: 250, Protein: 25g, Fat: 12g, Carbohydrates: 2g, Sugar: 1g

Quick tips:

- For a more intense flavor, marinate the fillets in the olive oil mixture for 30 minutes before air frying.
- Ensure the fillets are evenly spaced in the basket to promote even cooking.

Crispy Air Fried Clam Strips

Crispy Air Fried Clam Strips offer a delicious seafood appetizer with a crunchy coating and tender interior. This recipe provides a healthier alternative to deep-frying, perfect for enjoying as a snack or part of a main meal.

Tools needed:

- Ninja Air Fryer Pro
- Mixing bowls
- Air fryer basket
- Cooking spray

Ingredients:

- 1 pound clam strips, thawed if frozen
- 1/2 cup all-purpose flour
- 1/2 cup cornmeal
- 1/2 cup panko breadcrumbs
- 1 teaspoon Old Bay seasoning
- 1/2 teaspoon paprika
- 1/2 teaspoon garlic powder
- Salt and pepper to taste
- 2 large eggs, beaten
- Cooking spray

Direction:

1. Preheat the air fryer to 400°F (200°C).
2. Set up a breading station: Place flour in one bowl, beaten eggs in another, and a mixture of cornmeal, panko breadcrumbs, Old Bay seasoning, paprika, garlic powder, salt, and pepper in a third bowl.
3. Dredge each clam strip in flour, dip in the beaten eggs, and coat with the breadcrumb mixture.
4. Spray the air fryer basket with cooking spray and arrange the clam strips in a single layer.
5. Air fry for 8-10 minutes, or until golden brown and crispy, shaking the basket halfway through.
6. Serve with cocktail sauce or tartar sauce for dipping.

Servings: 4 | **Prep time:** 15 minutes | **Cooking time:** 8-10 minutes

Nutritional info (per serving, 6-8 clam strips): Calories: 250, Protein: 15g, Fat: 12g, Carbohydrates: 20g, Sugar: 2g
Quick tips:

- To avoid overcrowding, cook the clam strips in batches if necessary.
- For a touch of extra flavor, add a squeeze of lemon juice over the clam strips before serving.

AIRFRYER VEGETARIAN RECIPES

Air Fryer Stuffed Bell Peppers

Air Fryer Stuffed Bell Peppers are a nutritious and satisfying meal, with tender bell peppers filled with a flavorful mixture of ground meat, rice, and spices. This recipe makes use of the air fryer to cook the peppers evenly while keeping the stuffing moist and delicious.

Tools needed:

Ninja Air Fryer Pro
Mixing bowls
Air fryer basket
Cooking spray

Ingredients:

- 4 large bell peppers (any color)
- 1/2 pound ground beef or turkey
- 1/2 cup cooked rice
- 1/2 cup shredded cheese (cheddar or mozzarella)
- 1/2 cup diced tomatoes
- 1 small onion, diced
- 2 cloves garlic, minced
- 1 teaspoon dried oregano
- 1 teaspoon paprika
- Salt and pepper to taste
- Cooking spray

Direction:

1. Preheat the air fryer to 360°F (180°C).
2. Cut the tops off the bell peppers and remove the seeds and membranes.
3. In a skillet over medium heat, cook the ground beef or turkey with the onion and garlic until browned. Drain excess fat.
4. Stir in cooked rice, shredded cheese, diced tomatoes, oregano, paprika, salt, and pepper. Mix well.
5. Stuff each bell pepper with the meat mixture.
6. Spray the air fryer basket with cooking spray and arrange the stuffed peppers in a single layer.
7. Air fry for 12-15 minutes, or until the peppers are tender and the cheese is melted.
8. Serve warm.

Servings: 4 | **Prep time:** 15 minutes | **Cooking time:** 12-15 minutes

Nutritional info (per stuffed pepper):
Calories: 350
Protein: 20g
Fat: 18g
Carbohydrates: 30g
Sugar: 8g

Quick tips:

- For added flavor, top the stuffed peppers with a sprinkle of extra cheese before air frying.
- If the peppers are too large for the basket, you can cut them in half to fit.

Crispy Air Fried Cauliflower is a delicious and healthy alternative to traditional fried vegetables. The cauliflower florets are coated in a savory batter and air-fried to achieve a crunchy texture, making them a perfect snack or side dish.

Tools needed:

- Ninja Air Fryer Pro
- Mixing bowls
- Air fryer basket
- Cooking spray

Ingredients:

- 1 head cauliflower, cut into bite-sized florets
- 1/2 cup all-purpose flour
- 1/2 cup breadcrumbs
- 1/2 cup grated Parmesan cheese
- 1 teaspoon garlic powder
- 1 teaspoon onion powder
- 1/2 teaspoon paprika
- Salt and pepper to taste
- 2 large eggs, beaten
- Cooking spray

Direction:

1. Preheat the air fryer to 400°F (200°C).
2. In a bowl, mix flour, breadcrumbs, Parmesan cheese, garlic powder, onion powder, paprika, salt, and pepper.
3. Dip each cauliflower floret into the beaten eggs, then coat with the breadcrumb mixture.
4. Spray the air fryer basket with cooking spray and arrange the coated cauliflower in a single layer.
5. Air fry for 10-12 minutes, or until the cauliflower is golden brown and crispy, shaking the basket halfway through.
6. Serve warm with your favorite dipping sauce.

Servings: 4 | **Prep time:** 15 minutes | **Cooking time:** 10-12 minutes

Nutritional info (per serving, 1 cup): Calories: 180, Protein: 8g, Fat: 8g, Carbohydrates: 22g, Sugar: 5g

Quick tips:

- For extra crispiness, lightly spray the cauliflower with cooking spray before air frying.
- Adjust the seasoning to your taste; you can add a pinch of cayenne pepper for more heat.

Air Fryer Tofu Nuggets

Air Fryer Tofu Nuggets are a plant-based, crunchy snack or meal option. The tofu is marinated, breaded, and air-fried to perfection, providing a flavorful and satisfying alternative to traditional chicken nuggets.

Tools needed:

- Ninja Air Fryer Pro
- Mixing bowls
- Air fryer basket
- Cooking spray

Ingredients:

- 1 block firm tofu, drained and cubed
- 1/4 cup soy sauce
- 2 tablespoons rice vinegar
- 1 tablespoon sesame oil
- 1 tablespoon maple syrup
- 1/2 cup all-purpose flour
- 1/2 cup panko breadcrumbs
- 1 teaspoon garlic powder
- 1 teaspoon onion powder
- Salt and pepper to taste
- Cooking spray

Direction:

1. Preheat the air fryer to 375°F (190°C).
2. In a bowl, combine soy sauce, rice vinegar, sesame oil, and maple syrup. Add the tofu cubes and marinate for at least 15 minutes.
3. In a separate bowl, mix flour, panko breadcrumbs, garlic powder, onion powder, salt, and pepper.
4. Coat each tofu cube with the breadcrumb mixture.
5. Spray the air fryer basket with cooking spray and arrange the tofu nuggets in a single layer.
6. Air fry for 12-15 minutes, or until the tofu is golden brown and crispy, shaking the basket halfway through.
7. Serve with dipping sauce or a side salad.

Servings: 4 | **Prep time:** 20 minutes (including marination) | **Cooking time:** 12-15 minutes

Nutritional info (per serving, 5 nuggets): Calories: 220, Protein: 12g, Fat: 12g, Carbohydrates: 18g, Sugar: 3g
Quick tips:

- For a spicier kick, add a pinch of red pepper flakes to the breadcrumb mixture.
- Ensure the tofu is well-drained to achieve the best crispy texture.

Spicy Air Fried Chickpeas are a crunchy, flavorful snack that's easy to make and perfect for on-the-go munching. Seasoned with a mix of spices and air-fried to crisp perfection, these chickpeas are a great alternative to traditional chips.

Tools needed:

- Ninja Air Fryer Pro
- Mixing bowls
- Air fryer basket
- Cooking spray

Ingredients:

- 1 can (15 oz) chickpeas, drained and rinsed
- 1 tablespoon olive oil
- 1 teaspoon smoked paprika
- 1/2 teaspoon cayenne pepper
- 1/2 teaspoon garlic powder
- 1/2 teaspoon onion powder
- Salt to taste
- Cooking spray

Direction:

1. Preheat the air fryer to 400°F (200°C).
2. Pat the chickpeas dry with a paper towel.
3. In a bowl, toss the chickpeas with olive oil, smoked paprika, cayenne pepper, garlic powder, onion powder, and salt.
4. Spray the air fryer basket with cooking spray and add the seasoned chickpeas.
5. Air fry for 15-18 minutes, shaking the basket every 5 minutes, until the chickpeas are crispy.
6. Allow to cool slightly before serving. They will continue to crisp up as they cool.

Servings: 4 | **Prep time:** 5 minutes | **Cooking time:** 15-18 minutes

Nutritional info (per serving, 1/2 cup):
Calories: 180
Protein: 7g
Fat: 7g
Carbohydrates: 23g
Sugar: 2g

Quick tips:

- For extra crispiness, ensure chickpeas are completely dry before seasoning and air frying.
- Experiment with different spices to customize the flavor to your preference.

Air Fryer Eggplant Fries

Air Fryer Eggplant Fries are a crispy and healthy alternative to traditional potato fries. Coated in a seasoned breadcrumb mixture and air-fried, these eggplant fries offer a delicious, guilt-free snack or side dish.

Tools needed:

- Ninja Air Fryer Pro
- Mixing bowls
- Air fryer basket
- Cooking spray

Ingredients:

- 1 large eggplant, peeled and cut into fry-shaped pieces
- 1/2 cup all-purpose flour
- 1/2 cup panko breadcrumbs
- 1/4 cup grated Parmesan cheese
- 1 teaspoon garlic powder
- 1 teaspoon onion powder
- 1/2 teaspoon paprika
- Salt and pepper to taste
- 2 large eggs, beaten
- Cooking spray

Direction:

1. Preheat the air fryer to 400°F (200°C).
2. Set up a breading station: Place flour in one bowl, beaten eggs in another, and a mixture of panko breadcrumbs, Parmesan cheese, garlic powder, onion powder, paprika, salt, and pepper in a third bowl.
3. Dredge each eggplant fry in flour, dip in beaten eggs, and coat with the breadcrumb mixture.
4. Spray the air fryer basket with cooking spray and arrange the eggplant fries in a single layer.
5. Air fry for 10-12 minutes, or until golden brown and crispy, shaking the basket halfway through.
6. Serve with your favorite dipping sauce.

Servings: 4 | **Prep time:** 15 minutes | **Cooking time:** 10-12 minutes

Nutritional info (per serving, 1 cup): Calories: 150, Protein: 6g, Fat: 8g, Carbohydrates: 16g, Sugar: 6g

Quick tips:

- For extra crispiness, lightly spray the fries with cooking spray before air frying.
- Serve with a side of marinara sauce or garlic aioli for dipping.

Stuffed Portobello Mushrooms

Stuffed Portobello Mushrooms are a savory and satisfying dish, perfect as a main course or appetizer. The mushrooms are filled with a flavorful mixture of cheese, herbs, and breadcrumbs, then air-fried to create a crispy topping with a tender, juicy interior.

Tools needed:

- Ninja Air Fryer Pro
- Mixing bowls
- Air fryer basket
- Cooking spray

Ingredients:

- 4 large Portobello mushrooms, stems removed
- 1/2 cup cream cheese, softened
- 1/4 cup grated Parmesan cheese
- 1/4 cup shredded mozzarella cheese
- 1/4 cup breadcrumbs
- 1 teaspoon dried Italian herbs
- 1 clove garlic, minced
- Salt and pepper to taste
- Cooking spray

Direction:

1. Preheat the air fryer to 360°F (180°C).
2. In a bowl, mix cream cheese, Parmesan cheese, mozzarella cheese, breadcrumbs, Italian herbs, garlic, salt, and pepper.
3. Spoon the cheese mixture into the cavity of each mushroom cap.
4. Spray the air fryer basket with cooking spray and place the stuffed mushrooms in a single layer.
5. Air fry for 8-10 minutes, or until the cheese is melted and bubbly, and the mushrooms are tender.
6. Serve warm as an appetizer or side dish.

Servings: 4 | **Prep time:** 10 minutes | **Cooking time:** 8-10 minutes

Nutritional info (per mushroom): Calories: 200, Protein: 10g, Fat: 14g, Carbohydrates: 10g, Sugar: 3g

Quick tips:

- For added flavor, sprinkle a little extra Parmesan cheese on top of the mushrooms before air frying.
- Make sure to clean the mushroom caps thoroughly before stuffing.

Air Fried Vegetable Spring Rolls

Air Fried Vegetable Spring Rolls are a crispy, flavorful snack or appetizer, filled with a mix of fresh vegetables and seasoned with Asian-inspired spices. The air fryer makes them crispy without the need for deep frying, resulting in a healthier version of this classic dish.

Tools needed:

- Ninja Air Fryer Pro
- Mixing bowls
- Air fryer basket
- Cooking spray

Ingredients:

- 10-12 spring roll wrappers
- 1 cup shredded carrots
- 1 cup thinly sliced cabbage
- 1/2 cup sliced bell peppers
- 1/2 cup thinly sliced mushrooms
- 2 cloves garlic, minced
- 1 tablespoon soy sauce
- 1 teaspoon grated ginger
- 1 tablespoon vegetable oil
- Salt and pepper to taste
- Cooking spray

Direction:

1. Preheat the air fryer to 390°F (200°C).
2. In a bowl, mix shredded carrots, cabbage, bell peppers, mushrooms, garlic, soy sauce, ginger, vegetable oil, salt, and pepper.
3. Place a small amount of the vegetable mixture in the center of each spring roll wrapper. Fold in the sides and roll up tightly.
4. Spray the air fryer basket with cooking spray and arrange the spring rolls in a single layer.
5. Air fry for 8-10 minutes, or until golden brown and crispy, turning halfway through.
6. Serve with a side of sweet chili sauce or soy sauce for dipping.

Servings: 4 | **Prep time:** 20 minutes | **Cooking time:** 8-10 minutes

Nutritional info (per spring roll): Calories: 80, Protein: 2g, Fat: 3g, Carbohydrates: 10g, Sugar: 2g

Quick tips:

- Ensure the spring rolls are sealed tightly to prevent filling from spilling out during cooking.
- For extra crunch, lightly brush the spring rolls with vegetable oil before air frying.

Air Fryer Avocado Fries offer a creamy interior and a crispy exterior, making them a unique and delicious snack or side dish. Coated with a seasoned breadcrumb mixture and air-fried to perfection, these avocado fries are a healthy alternative to traditional fries.

Tools needed:

- Ninja Air Fryer Pro
- Mixing bowls
- Air fryer basket
- Cooking spray

Ingredients:

- 2 ripe avocados, peeled, pitted, and sliced into wedges
- 1/2 cup all-purpose flour
- 1/2 cup panko breadcrumbs
- 1/4 cup grated Parmesan cheese
- 1 teaspoon garlic powder
- 1 teaspoon onion powder
- 1/2 teaspoon paprika
- Salt and pepper to taste
- 2 large eggs, beaten
- Cooking spray

Direction:

1. Preheat the air fryer to 400°F (200°C).
2. Set up a breading station: Place flour in one bowl, beaten eggs in another, and a mixture of panko breadcrumbs, Parmesan cheese, garlic powder, onion powder, paprika, salt, and pepper in a third bowl.
3. Dredge each avocado wedge in flour, dip in beaten eggs, and coat with the breadcrumb mixture.
4. Spray the air fryer basket with cooking spray and arrange the avocado wedges in a single layer.
5. Air fry for 6-8 minutes, or until the avocado fries are golden brown and crispy, shaking the basket halfway through.
6. Serve with a side of ranch or aioli.

Servings: 4 | **Prep time:** 15 minutes | **Cooking time:** 6-8 minutes

Nutritional info (per serving, 4 wedges): Calories: 190, Protein: 6g, Fat: 14g, Carbohydrates: 16g, Sugar: 2g

Quick tips:

- Choose ripe avocados but not overly soft, as they need to hold their shape during cooking.
- For an extra crunch, lightly spray the avocado fries with cooking spray before air frying.

Crispy Brussels Sprouts

Crispy Brussels Sprouts are a flavorful and nutritious side dish, featuring a crunchy exterior and tender interior. Air frying these sprouts enhances their natural sweetness while adding a satisfying crispiness.

Tools needed:

- Ninja Air Fryer Pro
- Mixing bowls
- Air fryer basket
- Cooking spray

Ingredients:

- 1 pound Brussels sprouts, trimmed and halved
- 2 tablespoons olive oil
- 1 teaspoon garlic powder
- 1 teaspoon onion powder
- 1/2 teaspoon smoked paprika
- Salt and pepper to taste
- Cooking spray

Direction:

1. Preheat the air fryer to 375°F (190°C).
2. In a bowl, toss Brussels sprouts with olive oil, garlic powder, onion powder, smoked paprika, salt, and pepper.
3. Spray the air fryer basket with cooking spray and add the Brussels sprouts in a single layer.
4. Air fry for 15-18 minutes, shaking the basket halfway through, until the sprouts are crispy and golden brown.
5. Serve immediately, optionally with a sprinkle of Parmesan cheese or a squeeze of lemon.

Servings: 4 | **Prep time:** 10 minutes | **Cooking time:** 15-18 minutes

Nutritional info (per serving, 1 cup):
Calories: 120
Protein: 4g
Fat: 8g
Carbohydrates: 12g
Sugar: 2g

Quick tips:

- For extra crispy sprouts, make sure they are spread out in a single layer in the air fryer basket.
- Adjust the seasoning to your taste; a pinch of red pepper flakes can add a nice kick.

Air Fried Vegetable Skewers are a versatile and healthy option for a quick meal or appetizer. The combination of vibrant vegetables is seasoned and air-fried to create a deliciously crispy exterior with tender, flavorful insides.

Tools needed:

- Ninja Air Fryer Pro
- Skewers
- Mixing bowls
- Air fryer basket
- Cooking spray

Ingredients:

- 1 bell pepper, cut into chunks
- 1 zucchini, sliced
- 1 red onion, cut into chunks
- 1 cup cherry tomatoes
- 1 cup mushrooms, whole or halved
- 2 tablespoons olive oil
- 1 teaspoon dried oregano
- 1 teaspoon garlic powder
- 1/2 teaspoon paprika
- Salt and pepper to taste
- Cooking spray

Direction:

1. Preheat the air fryer to 400°F (200°C).
2. In a bowl, toss the vegetables with olive oil, oregano, garlic powder, paprika, salt, and pepper.
3. Thread the vegetables onto skewers, alternating the types.
4. Spray the air fryer basket with cooking spray and place the skewers in a single layer.
5. Air fry for 8-10 minutes, turning the skewers halfway through, until the vegetables are tender and slightly charred.
6. Serve warm, optionally with a side of tzatziki or hummus.

Servings: 4 | **Prep time:** 15 minutes | **Cooking time:** 8-10 minutes

Nutritional info (per serving, 2 skewers): Calories: 120, Protein: 3g, Fat: 8g, Carbohydrates: 12g, Sugar: 5g

Quick tips:

- Soak wooden skewers in water for 30 minutes before using to prevent them from burning.
- Feel free to mix and match vegetables according to your preference or what's in season.

AIRFRYER DESSERTS RECIPES

Air Fryer Churros

Air Fryer Churros offer the classic crispy, cinnamon-sugar treat with less oil and mess. These churros are perfectly golden and crunchy on the outside while remaining soft and delicious on the inside.

Tools needed:

- Ninja Air Fryer Pro
- Piping bag or plastic sandwich bag
- Mixing bowls
- Air fryer basket
- Cooking spray

Ingredients:

- 1 cup water
- 1/2 cup unsalted butter
- 1 tablespoon granulated sugar
- 1/4 teaspoon salt
- 1 cup all-purpose flour
- 2 large eggs
- 1/2 cup granulated sugar (for coating)
- 1 teaspoon ground cinnamon (for coating)
- Cooking spray

Direction:

1. Preheat the air fryer to 375°F (190°C).
2. In a saucepan over medium heat, bring water, butter, sugar, and salt to a boil.
3. Remove from heat and stir in flour until well combined. Let the mixture cool slightly.
4. Beat in the eggs, one at a time, until smooth and doughy.
5. Transfer the dough to a piping bag fitted with a large star tip.
6. Pipe churro shapes onto parchment paper, cut to desired lengths.
7. Spray the air fryer basket with cooking spray and place churros in a single layer.
8. Air fry for 8-10 minutes, or until golden brown and crispy.
9. Mix granulated sugar and cinnamon in a bowl. Roll the churros in the cinnamon sugar mixture before serving.

Servings: 6 | **Prep time:** 20 minutes | **Cooking time:** 8-10 minutes

Nutritional info (per churro, approx. 4 inches): Calories: 120, Protein: 2g, Fat: 7g, Carbohydrates: 15g, Sugar: 8g
Quick tips:

- Ensure churros are not overcrowded in the air fryer basket for even cooking.
- For extra flavor, you can add a drizzle of chocolate or caramel sauce

Air Fried Apple Pies are a delightful, mini dessert that combines a crispy exterior with a sweet, spiced apple filling. These mini pies are perfect for a quick treat or dessert.

Tools needed:

- Ninja Air Fryer Pro
- Rolling pin
- Mixing bowls
- Air fryer basket
- Cooking spray

Ingredients:

- 1 sheet store-bought pie dough
- 2 medium apples, peeled and diced
- 1/4 cup granulated sugar
- 1/2 teaspoon ground cinnamon
- 1/4 teaspoon ground nutmeg
- 1 tablespoon all-purpose flour
- 1 egg, beaten (for egg wash)
- Cooking spray

Direction:

1. Preheat the air fryer to 375°F (190°C).
2. In a bowl, mix diced apples, sugar, cinnamon, nutmeg, and flour until well combined.
3. Roll out the pie dough on a floured surface and cut into 4-inch squares or circles.
4. Place a spoonful of the apple mixture in the center of each dough piece.
5. Fold the dough over the filling to form a triangle or half-moon shape, sealing the edges with a fork.
6. Brush the tops with beaten egg and spray lightly with cooking spray.
7. Air fry for 10-12 minutes, or until golden brown and crispy.
8. Allow to cool slightly before serving.

Servings: 4 | **Prep time:** 20 minutes | **Cooking time:** 10-12 minutes

Nutritional info (per pie):
Calories: 210
Protein: 2g
Fat: 11g
Carbohydrates: 27g
Sugar: 12g

Quick tips:

- For a caramelized finish, sprinkle a little extra sugar on top of the pies before air frying.
- Serve with a scoop of vanilla ice cream for an extra treat.

Chocolate Lava Cakes

Chocolate Lava Cakes are a decadent dessert with a gooey chocolate center that flows when you cut into them. Made in the air fryer, these individual cakes are easy to prepare and perfect for any special occasion.

Tools needed:

- Ninja Air Fryer Pro
- Ramekins
- Mixing bowls
- Air fryer basket
- Cooking spray

Ingredients:

- 1/2 cup unsalted butter
- 1 cup semi-sweet chocolate chips
- 1 cup powdered sugar
- 2 large eggs
- 2 large egg yolks
- 1 teaspoon vanilla extract
- 1/2 cup all-purpose flour
- Cooking spray

Direction:

1. Preheat the air fryer to 360°F (180°C).
2. In a microwave-safe bowl, melt butter and chocolate chips together in 30-second intervals, stirring until smooth.
3. Stir in powdered sugar until combined. Add eggs and egg yolks, mixing well.
4. Mix in vanilla extract and flour until just combined.
5. Spray ramekins with cooking spray and divide the batter evenly among them.
6. Air fry for 8-10 minutes, or until the edges are set but the centers are still soft.
7. Let the cakes cool for 1 minute before inverting onto plates.
8. Serve warm, optionally dusted with powdered sugar or topped with berries.

Servings: 4 | **Prep time:** 15 minutes | **Cooking time:** 8-10 minutes

Nutritional info (per cake): Calories: 380, Protein: 6g, Fat: 24g, Carbohydrates: 37g, Sugar: 28g

Quick tips:

- Serve immediately to enjoy the molten center.
- For a smoother lava center, ensure the cakes are slightly undercooked in the center.

Air Fryer Donut Holes are bite-sized, fluffy treats coated in cinnamon sugar. These mini donuts are light, delicious, and easy to make, offering a perfect snack or dessert with less oil than traditional frying.

Tools needed:

- Ninja Air Fryer Pro
- Mixing bowls
- Air fryer basket
- Piping bag or plastic sandwich bag
- Cooking spray

Ingredients:

- 1 cup all-purpose flour
- 1/4 cup granulated sugar
- 1 1/2 teaspoons baking powder
- 1/4 teaspoon salt
- 1/2 cup milk
- 1 large egg
- 2 tablespoons unsalted butter, melted
- 1 teaspoon vanilla extract
- 1/4 cup granulated sugar (for coating)
- 1 teaspoon ground cinnamon (for coating)
- Cooking spray

Direction:

1. Preheat the air fryer to 350°F (175°C).
2. In a bowl, whisk together flour, sugar, baking powder, and salt.
3. In another bowl, combine milk, egg, melted butter, and vanilla extract.
4. Mix wet ingredients into the dry ingredients until just combined.
5. Transfer the batter to a piping bag or plastic sandwich bag and cut off a small corner.
6. Pipe small dollops of batter into the air fryer basket, ensuring they are spaced apart.
7. Spray the batter with cooking spray and air fry for 6-8 minutes, or until golden brown.
8. Mix granulated sugar and cinnamon in a bowl. Roll the warm donut holes in the cinnamon sugar mixture before serving.

Servings: 4 | **Prep time:** 10 minutes | **Cooking time:** 6-8 minutes

Nutritional info (per donut hole, approx. 1 inch): Calories: 60, Protein: 1g, Fat: 2g, Carbohydrates: 10g, Sugar: 5g

Quick tips:

- To ensure even cooking, avoid overcrowding the air fryer basket.
- For an extra touch, drizzle with a simple glaze made from powdered sugar and milk.

Cinnamon Sugar Air Fried Bananas

Cinnamon Sugar Air Fried Bananas are a simple yet delightful dessert. The bananas are coated in a sweet cinnamon sugar mixture and air-fried to caramelized perfection, making for a warm, comforting treat.

Tools needed:

- Ninja Air Fryer Pro
- Mixing bowls
- Air fryer basket
- Cooking spray

Ingredients:

- 2 ripe bananas, peeled and sliced into 1/2-inch rounds
- 1/4 cup granulated sugar
- 1 teaspoon ground cinnamon
- Cooking spray

Direction:

1. Preheat the air fryer to 370°F (190°C).
2. In a bowl, mix granulated sugar and cinnamon.
3. Toss banana slices in the cinnamon sugar mixture until well coated.
4. Spray the air fryer basket with cooking spray and arrange the banana slices in a single layer.
5. Air fry for 5-7 minutes, or until the bananas are golden and caramelized, shaking the basket halfway through.
6. Serve warm, optionally with a scoop of ice cream or a drizzle of honey.

Servings: 2 | **Prep time:** 5 minutes | **Cooking time:** 5-7 minutes

Nutritional info (per serving, 1/2 banana):
Calories: 80
Protein: 1g
Fat: 0g
Carbohydrates: 21g
Sugar: 14g

Quick tips:

- Ensure bananas are sliced evenly for consistent cooking.
- Serve immediately for the best texture and flavor.

Air Fryer Brownies are rich, fudgy, and incredibly easy to make. This recipe delivers deliciously gooey brownies with a slightly crispy edge, all done in the air fryer for a quick and convenient treat.

Tools needed:

- Ninja Air Fryer Pro
- Mixing bowls
- Air fryer-safe baking pan or ramekins
- Cooking spray

Ingredients:

- 1/2 cup unsalted butter
- 1 cup granulated sugar
- 1/2 cup cocoa powder
- 2 large eggs
- 1/2 teaspoon vanilla extract
- 1/2 cup all-purpose flour
- 1/4 teaspoon salt
- 1/4 teaspoon baking powder
- Cooking spray

Direction:

1. Preheat the air fryer to 320°F (160°C).
2. In a microwave-safe bowl, melt butter and whisk in granulated sugar and cocoa powder until smooth.
3. Beat in eggs, one at a time, then stir in vanilla extract.
4. Mix in flour, salt, and baking powder until just combined.
5. Spray the air fryer-safe baking pan or ramekins with cooking spray and pour in the brownie batter.
6. Air fry for 15-18 minutes, or until a toothpick inserted into the center comes out with a few moist crumbs.
7. Allow to cool slightly before slicing and serving.

Servings: 4 | **Prep time:** 10 minutes | **Cooking time:** 15-18 minutes

Nutritional info (per brownie, 1/4 of the batch): Calories: 230, Protein: 3g, Fat: 14g, Carbohydrates: 25g, Sugar: 19g

Quick tips:

- Check brownies a few minutes before the end of the cooking time to avoid overbaking.
- Let brownies cool completely before cutting to help them set properly.

Crispy Air Fried Cheesecake Bites

Crispy Air Fried Cheesecake Bites offer a delightful twist on classic cheesecake. These mini treats have a crisp exterior with a creamy, rich filling inside, all made with less oil than traditional frying.

Tools needed:

- Ninja Air Fryer Pro
- Mixing bowls
- Air fryer basket
- Cooking spray
- Toothpicks or skewers (optional)

Ingredients:

- 1 cup cream cheese, softened
- 1/2 cup granulated sugar
- 1/2 teaspoon vanilla extract
- 1 large egg
- 1 cup graham cracker crumbs
- 1/4 cup granulated sugar (for coating)
- Cooking spray

Direction:

1. Preheat the air fryer to 350°F (175°C).
2. In a bowl, mix cream cheese, sugar, and vanilla extract until smooth.
3. Beat in the egg until well combined.
4. Refrigerate the cheesecake mixture for about 30 minutes to firm up.
5. Shape the chilled mixture into small balls and coat each ball with graham cracker crumbs.
6. Spray the air fryer basket with cooking spray and place the cheesecake bites in a single layer.
7. Air fry for 6-8 minutes, or until the coating is golden brown and crispy.
8. Allow to cool slightly before serving. Optionally, use toothpicks for easy serving.

Servings: 6 | **Prep time:** 20 minutes | **Cooking time:** 6-8 minutes

Nutritional info (per bite, approx. 1 inch): Calories: 100, Protein: 2g, Fat: 7g, Carbohydrates: 8g, Sugar: 5g

Quick tips:

- For a smoother coating, press the graham cracker crumbs gently onto the cheesecake balls before air frying.
- Serve with a drizzle of chocolate or caramel sauce for extra indulgence.

Air Fried S'mores bring the classic campfire treat into the kitchen with a crispy, warm exterior and gooey, melty filling. This easy recipe is perfect for a quick dessert fix.

Tools needed:

- Ninja Air Fryer Pro
- Mixing bowls
- Air fryer basket
- Cooking spray

Ingredients:

- 4 graham crackers, broken into squares
- 4 large marshmallows
- 4 squares milk chocolate or chocolate bar pieces
- Cooking spray

Direction:

1. Preheat the air fryer to 350°F (175°C).
2. Place a piece of chocolate on top of a graham cracker square.
3. Place a marshmallow on top of the chocolate, and then cover with another graham cracker square.
4. Spray the air fryer basket lightly with cooking spray and arrange the s'mores in a single layer.
5. Air fry for 4-5 minutes, or until the marshmallows are golden and the chocolate is melted.
6. Allow to cool slightly before serving.

Servings: 4 | **Prep time:** 5 minutes | **Cooking time:** 4-5 minutes

Nutritional info (per s'more):
Calories: 200
Protein: 2g
Fat: 9g
Carbohydrates: 29g
Sugar: 18g

Quick tips:

- Keep an eye on the s'mores as they cook to prevent burning.
- For a fun twist, add a layer of peanut butter or caramel between the chocolate and marshmallow.

Blueberry Air Fryer Muffins are fluffy, moist, and packed with juicy blueberries. They are a perfect breakfast or snack option, cooked quickly and easily in the air fryer.

Tools needed:

- Ninja Air Fryer Pro
- Mixing bowls
- Muffin liners or silicone muffin cups
- Air fryer basket

Ingredients:

- 1 cup all-purpose flour
- 1/2 cup granulated sugar
- 1/2 teaspoon baking powder
- 1/4 teaspoon baking soda
- 1/4 teaspoon salt
- 1/2 cup milk
- 1/4 cup vegetable oil
- 1 large egg
- 1 teaspoon vanilla extract
- 1 cup fresh or frozen blueberries
- Cooking spray

Direction:

1. Preheat the air fryer to 320°F (160°C).
2. In a bowl, mix flour, sugar, baking powder, baking soda, and salt.
3. In another bowl, whisk together milk, vegetable oil, egg, and vanilla extract.
4. Combine the wet and dry ingredients until just mixed. Gently fold in the blueberries.
5. Line the air fryer basket with muffin liners or use silicone muffin cups.
6. Divide the batter evenly among the muffin cups.
7. Air fry for 10-12 minutes, or until a toothpick inserted into the center comes out clean.
8. Allow to cool slightly before serving.

Servings: 6 | **Prep time:** 10 minutes | **Cooking time:** 10-12 minutes

Nutritional info (per muffin): Calories: 150, Protein: 3g, Fat: 6g, Carbohydrates: 22g, Sugar: 11g

Quick tips:

- If using frozen blueberries, do not thaw them to prevent the batter from turning blue.
- For added flavor, sprinkle a bit of sugar on top of the muffins before air frying.

Peanut Butter Cookies

Air Fried Peanut Butter Cookies are a classic treat with a delicious twist. These cookies are perfectly crispy on the outside and soft on the inside, all made with less oil thanks to the air fryer. They offer a quick and easy way to satisfy your sweet tooth.

Tools needed:

- Ninja Air Fryer Pro
- Mixing bowls
- Air fryer basket
- Cooking spray
- Cookie scoop or tablespoon

Ingredients:

- 1 cup creamy peanut butter
- 1 cup granulated sugar
- 1 large egg
- 1/2 teaspoon vanilla extract
- 1/2 teaspoon baking soda
- A pinch of salt
- Additional granulated sugar for rolling

Direction:

1. Preheat the air fryer to 350°F (175°C).
2. In a bowl, mix peanut butter, sugar, egg, vanilla extract, baking soda, and salt until smooth.
3. Scoop tablespoon-sized balls of dough and roll them in additional granulated sugar.
4. Flatten each cookie ball slightly with a fork to create a crisscross pattern.
5. Spray the air fryer basket with cooking spray and arrange the cookies in a single layer, leaving space between them.
6. Air fry for 6-8 minutes, or until the cookies are golden brown and set.
7. Allow to cool in the basket for a few minutes before transferring to a wire rack to cool completely.

Servings: 12 | **Prep time:** 10 minutes | **Cooking time:** 6-8 minutes

Nutritional info (per cookie): Calories: 120, Protein: 3g, Fat: 9g, Carbohydrates: 9g, Sugar: 8g

Quick tips:

- For best results, make sure the dough balls are evenly sized for consistent cooking.
- If you like extra crunch, add chopped peanuts or a sprinkle of sea salt on top before air frying.

CONCLUSION

Congratulations on completing your journey through the Ninja Air Fryer Pro cookbook! You've now learned how to use this versatile appliance to create a wide range of delicious, healthy meals. The possibilities are endless, and the only limit is your imagination.

As you continue to explore the capabilities of your Ninja Air Fryer Pro, don't be afraid to experiment with new ingredients and recipes. This appliance is designed to make cooking fun, easy, and rewarding. Whether you're trying out a new marinade, exploring different cooking techniques, or simply tweaking a favorite recipe, enjoy the process and savor the results. Each culinary adventure brings you one step closer to mastering your air fryer.

Remember a few key tips for ongoing success. Always preheat your air fryer for optimal results and keep an eye on your food as it cooks to ensure perfect doneness. For even cooking, it's important to shake the basket or rotate the food halfway through the cooking process. Regular cleaning of the basket and crisper plate will prevent residue buildup and ensure consistent performance. Additionally, take advantage of the accessories included with your air fryer, such as the crisper plate, to enhance your cooking experience and expand your recipe repertoire.

One of the joys of using the Ninja Air Fryer Pro is the ability to cook healthier meals without compromising on taste and texture. With up to 75% less fat than traditional frying methods, you can enjoy guilt-free fried foods that are crispy on the outside and tender on the inside. Plus, the convenience of cooking from frozen to crispy in just minutes makes it easier than ever to prepare quick and satisfying meals.

Embrace the space-saving design of your Ninja Air Fryer Pro, which allows you to enjoy all its features without taking up too much countertop space. This compact yet powerful appliance is perfect for any kitchen, big or small, and its easy-to-clean components make post-cooking cleanup a breeze.

As you continue to explore the recipes and techniques in this cookbook, you'll gain confidence in your cooking skills and find yourself experimenting more and more. Whether you're making a quick weeknight dinner, a special weekend brunch, or an indulgent dessert, the Ninja Air Fryer Pro is your trusted companion in the kitchen.

Thank you for being a part of this culinary journey. Your Ninja Air Fryer Pro is more than just an appliance—it's a gateway to endless delicious possibilities. So go ahead, get creative, and most importantly, have fun. Happy cooking!

2-WEEK MEAL PLAN

Day	Breakfast	Lunch	Dinner	Snack/Dessert
Monday	Air Fried Avocado Toast	Air Fried Greek Potatoes	Air Fried Buffalo Drumsticks	Air Fryer Churros
Tuesday	Breakfast Egg Muffins	Beef Stroganoff	Air Fryer Pork Schnitzel	Air Fried S'mores
Wednesday	Sweet Potato Breakfast Fries	Air Fried Steak Bites	Chicken Tikka Masala	Air Fryer Brownies
Thursday	Air Fried Oatmeal Cups	Air Fryer Stuffed Bell Peppers	Air Fried Calamari	Air Fried Pretzel Bites
Friday	Apple Cinnamon Breakfast Donuts	Air Fryer Cheeseburger Sliders	Air Fried Lamb Shawarma	Crispy Air Fried Cheesecake Bites
Saturday	Air Fryer French Toast Sticks	Air Fried Chicken Wontons	Air Fryer Cilantro Lime Chicken	Air Fried Apple Pies
Sunday	Blueberry Air Fryer Muffins	BBQ Pulled Pork Sandwiches	Moroccan Spiced Air Fryer Lamb	Air Fried Spanakopita
Monday	Banana Bread Bites	Beef Taquitos	Lemon Herb Air Fryer Chicken Breast	Peanut Butter Cookies

Tuesday	Breakfast Burrito Pockets	Air Fryer Coconut Shrimp	Air Fried Lamb Meatballs	Air Fried Onion Rings
Wednesday	Crispy Breakfast Hash Browns	Air Fryer Pork Belly Bites	Air Fried Beef Chimichangas	Air Fryer Mozzarella Sticks
Thursday	Air Fryer Cinnamon Rolls	Air Fryer Mahi Mahi	Greek Lemon Chicken Skewers	Cinnamon Sugar Air Fried Bananas
Friday	Breakfast Egg Muffins	Air Fried Crab Cakes	Spicy Lamb Kebabs	Air Fryer Donut Holes
Saturday	Air Fried Oatmeal Cups	Mongolian Beef Strips	Garlic Herb Air Fried Shrimp	Crispy Air Fried Cauliflower
Sunday	Sweet Potato Breakfast Fries	Mediterranean Chicken Meatballs	Honey Garlic Chicken Thighs	Air Fried Tofu Nuggets

RECIPE INDEX

Made in United States
Troutdale, OR
01/09/2025

27783760R00071